ASPECTS OF CHRISTIAN INTEGRITY

Aspects
of
Christian Integrity

Alan P. F. Sell

Westminster/John Knox Press
Louisville, Kentucky

First published in 1990
by the University of Calgary Press

Copyright © 1990 Alan P. F. Sell

Scripture quotations from the Revised Standard Version of the Bible are copyright 1946, 1952, © 1971, 1973 by the Division of Christian Education of the National Council of the Churches of Christ in the U.S.A. and are used by permission.

First United States edition

Published by Westminster / John Knox Press
Louisville, Kentucky

PRINTED IN THE UNITED STATES OF AMERICA
9 8 7 6 5 4 3 2 1

Library of Congress Cataloging-in-Publication Data

Sell, Alan P. F.
   Aspects of Christian integrity / Alan P. F. Sell—1st U.S. ed.
      p.   cm.
   Includes bibliographical references and indexes.
   ISBN 0-664-25245-1

   I. Title.
BV4647.I55S44 1990
241'.4—dc20   91-21693

To My Friends
of Town and Gown
in Calgary

CONTENTS

PREFACE

Integrity is an ambiguous term. Its principal meanings are honesty and wholeness. In neither of its main senses is integrity a uniquely Christian virtue or characteristic. Non-Christian individuals, institutions and communities can be honest, and can display wholeness. Conversely, Christians can be dishonest and, for example, the primary Christian institution, the visible Church, is marked by serious disunity. All the more reason, therefore, to examine what honesty and wholeness do and might mean in relation to Christian faith and practice.

The ambiguous nature of integrity is exploited in this series of lectures. Integrity in the sense of honesty is a central theme in the fifth lecture, where the question in a nutshell is, "Can Christians with integrity undertake a mission to the whole world?" In the second and sixth lectures, integrity as wholeness is foremost: "How far ought the several Christian doctrines to be regarded as constituting a systematic whole? What may we understand by whole churches ministered to by whole ministers performing a whole ministry?" The first, third and fourth lectures illustrate the point that in the fields of Christian thought, ethics and ecclesiology issues of honesty and wholeness overlap in sometimes quite complicated ways.

The lectures here offered to a wider audience were given under the auspices of the Chair of Christian Thought in the University of Calgary. This Chair, a co-operative venture on the part of the University and a number of Canadian churches, is the only one of its kind in Canada. The terms of reference of the Chair require the occupant to undertake research and writing, to teach within the Department of Religious Studies, and to serve the local and wider Christian communities in a variety of theological ways. The prescribed aspect of the third category of work is the delivery of Public Lectures.

I have found it challenging to attempt to catch the interest of the diverse, and encouragingly large, audiences which have attended the lectures. The humble believer, the "practising parson," the academic theologian, scholars from many disciplines — not excluding a leaven of (at least) professional sceptics — have all been present. I hope that all have gained something — even if only ammunition — from what, in hour-long lectures, could be only scratchings of the surface.

Four of the lectures are named in honour of those whose commitment and generosity ensured the establishment of the Chair: Howard Bentall, Kaz Iwaasa, J. Lewis Lebel and Archdeacon Cecil Swanson. Appropriately enough, these benefactors represent the Baptist, United, Roman Catholic and Anglican traditions respectively.

The Chair committee decided that the lectures should alternate between University and church venues. Thus, the first, third and fifth lectures were given at the University, and the topics on those occasions were somewhat less confessional than those treated on church premises. The second lecture was delivered at Knox United Church, Calgary, the fourth at St. Peter's Anglican Church, Calgary, and the sixth at First Baptist Church, Calgary. I am grateful to the respective ministers, the Reverend Grant Dawson, Archdeacon Robert Pynn, the Reverend Dr. Roy Bell (now of Vancouver) and the Reverend Dr. Douglas Moffat for their cordial co-operation and hospitality. Thanks are also due to Dr. Merlin B. Brinkerhoff, Associate Vice-President (Research), for chairing one of the sessions; and to the Reverend Dr. Harold G. Coward, Director of the University of Calgary Institute for the Humanities, Dr. Ronald W. Neufeldt, Head of the Department of Religious Studies, and Dr. Howard Bentall, formerly of First Baptist Church, Calgary, for chairing other sessions.

Some of the material here published has been tested elsewhere. I was first prompted to reflect upon the ambiguities of integrity by the [British] Society for the Study of Theology, before whom I delivered a paper on "Ecclesiastical integrity and failure" at Cambridge in April 1987. I thank the Committee of the Society for their kind invitation. The substance of lectures two and six became two of the four G. K. Simpson Lectures which I gave at Acadia Divinity College, Acadia University, in February 1989. Hearty thanks are due to the Reverend Dr. Andrew MacRae, Principal of the College, for the privilege of contributing to this important series of lectures, and to his wife, Jean, and other colleagues, for generously opening their homes to me. The gist of the third lecture was presented at the annual meeting of the Society of Christian Philosophers (Canadian Branch), at the University of Laval, in May 1989. For this invitation I am indebted to Professor Harold Johnson and the Committee of the Society. Lectures three to six were repeated at Medicine Hat College, Alberta, in January 1990, and I warmly thank the Board of the College and the Medicine Hat Ministerial, and especially the Reverend David W. Paterson, for this opportunity. Parts of the material here presented have been heard and debated by audiences at the Andover Newton Theological School, the Presbyterian College, Montreal, and at Pendle Hill, a Quaker Center for Study and Contemplation. For these invitations I am indebted to Professor Gabriel Fackre, Principal William Klempa and Margery Walker respectively.

My final word of thanks is to Linda Cameron and her colleagues at the University of Calgary Press for their courtesy and promptness in all matters pertaining to the publication of this book.

Alan P.F. Sell
The University of Calgary

This book has been published with the help of a grant from the Alberta Foundation for the Literary Arts.

THE INTEGRITY OF CHRISTIAN THOUGHT

THE INTEGRITY OF CHRISTIAN THOUGHT

The Howard Bentall Lecture

The process of establishing the Chair of Christian Thought at the University of Calgary was begun in 1979. The University and the Calgary Inter-Faith Community Action Organization are partners in the venture, and tribute must be paid to Dr. J. Louis Lebel and others, under whose leadership many groups and individuals contributed sufficient funds to inaugurate the Chair in 1986.

The first Chairholder was the Reverend Professor H. Gordon Harland, of the University of Manitoba, whose tenure lasted for two terms (1986–87). Professor Harland was indefatigable in his efforts to make the new Chair known in the vicinity, and his public lectures, now published,[1] and class teaching were much appreciated.

I regard it as an honour to have been invited to occupy this Chair, which is unique in Canada. The challenge of balancing the three main terms of reference: postgraduate teaching, research and writing, and the theological "infiltration" of the local and wider communities is as awesome as it is exciting. Needless to say, I have not arrived here unaided. You must therefore allow me a one-sentence tribute to parents and ministers, and to teachers, students and colleagues around the world, from whom I have received so much encouragement over the years. Nor do I take for granted the fact that my wife has, for the fifth time, uncomplainingly allowed herself to be uprooted, and her musical career to be interrupted, as we have traversed half the world to our third country of residence. The consciousness of support-from-afar of children and grandchildren is a further consolation. The cordial welcome we have received from University colleagues and churches alike is something for which we are deeply grateful.

3

This series of public lectures from the Chair has the title, *Aspects of Christian Integrity*. Under this heading I shall be able to offer some reflections upon important issues. I shall also be able to embrace at least some of the concerns of those who have endowed a number of the lectures. My inaugural lecture is on "The Integrity of Christian Thought" and it is this year's Howard Bentall Lecture.

The title is splendidly ambiguous! The terms "integrity" and "Christian Thought" have more than one meaning. Integrity signifies both honesty and wholeness, and Christian Thought denotes an academic discipline whose literature is open to Christians and non-Christians alike, as well as the processes and results of the mental activity of Christians of all kinds. Again, the term Christian Thought can be used descriptively to distinguish an example of Christian intellectual activity from that of another faith. In this sense, a book by the Archbishop of Canterbury would exemplify Christian thought in a way that a book by the Chief Rabbi would not. Yet again, Christian thought can have a moral connotation — like Christian behaviour. The context would normally make it clear that by Christian thought is intended "worthy thought." On this interpretation Christians themselves are prone to thinking unchristian thoughts: hence the Apostle Paul's declaration that he strives to "compel every human thought to surrender in obedience to Christ" (II Cor. 10:5).

 I

Let us think first of the academic discipline of Christian Thought. What are some of its ingredients? There is, in the first place, the history of Christian thought. We now have almost two thousand years of this history, and its roots go still further back. The years have bequeathed us a vast amount of literature. We can, for example, trace the relations between Christian thought and the general intellectual environment at particular periods. Sometimes, and in the case of some writers, it is difficult to distinguish between philosophy and theology, for philosophy is regarded as the handmaid of theology. At other times, and in some writers, there may be a severance of relations between Christian and other thought, as when Christians encapsulate their thought within a circle of revelation in such a way that conversation with philosophy ceases; or when secular philosophers, under the influence of logical positivism, proscribe religious discourse on the ground of its meaninglessness, or because of its alleged "non-falsifiability." More generally, Christian Thought as a subject of academic study encompasses Christian reflection upon morality and art, culture, politics and science. Let it not be forgotten, for example, that a powerful stimulus to the rise of modern science was the religious desire to explore what was deemed to *God*'s handiwork.

Next, there is the history and analysis of Christian doctrine, with all its schools of thought and varieties of expression. We can study the forging of the doctrine of the Trinity in the early centuries of the Christian era; we can examine the reconstruction of the doctrine of creation in the wake of the deliverances of modern science. Again, on the basis of the Bible, and with reference to the extending (I do not use the value-laden term, "developing") tradition, many have attempted systematic theologies. Older writers used to refer to the major themes within systematics as departments: God (including creation and the Trinity); humanity and sin; the remedy for sin in the person and work of Christ; the Church as the community of the redeemed; and eschatology — the last things: heaven, hell, death and judgment. Before the rise of modern Biblical criticism, and sometimes even after that rise, systematicians would plunder the Bible, in what we should now regard as an indiscriminate way, for their proof texts. Moreover, some were too easily convinced that the Bible yielded but one way of putting things — namely, their own! Their quest was for integrity in the sense of wholeness: they sought a rounded and complete system of Bible-grounded teaching; but some of their procedures, if pursued today, would be deemed to lack integrity in the sense of honesty *vis à vis* the Biblical text.

Under the heading "Philosophical Theology" we find attempts to articulate a Christian view of the world — normally in relation to prevailing tendencies in the current intellectual environment. Thus, for example, we find idealist, existentialist and process adumbrations of Christian themes. The question of the method which may appropriately be adopted in such work is complex indeed, and I shall have a little more to say about it towards the end of this lecture. Meanwhile, I would note that such tantalizing issues as the existence of God, the problem of evil — in particular, the question, Why do the righteous suffer?, the puzzles surrounding the ideas of resurrection and immortality, and the relation between faith and reason — all of these and many more persist through the ages, and to these the philosopher of religion, believer or not, devotes attention. Underlying all is the question of the bases and presuppositions of Christian thought. Is it founded upon the Bible? If so, in what way? Does it depend upon the authority of the Church? If so, what is the nature of that authority, and how is it exercized? Or are we dependent upon the individual's conscience or religious experience? If so, can what is said have anything other than the status of autobiographical testimony, which we are expected to take or leave without grounds?

From this very brief survey of an intellectual territory it is clear that Christian thought as a discipline has its history, its literature, its manifold aspects, and its perennial problems. Its detailed study requires classical and modern languages, an acquaintance with historical methods, and the development of philosophical and analytical skills — all of this together with sensitivity to issues of many kinds, and to convictions, some of which may be alien or even repugnant to the student. A course in Christian Thought cannot hope to have integrity in the sense of wholeness if by that we mean that it will treat all the Christian thinking there ever was. For one thing, life is short; for another, there is the matter of lost manuscripts. But such a course should at least include a range of materials written in different styles, and requiring a variety of skills for their assessment. It is my conviction that the study of Christian thought can and should foster many of the ingredients of a liberal education, if such an education is defined as including the understanding and critique of culture, and the development of linguistic, literary and critical skills.

Sadly, however, the holder of a Chair of Christian Thought cannot expect everyone to agree. Holders of University Chairs whose products are manifestly useful, or technically or mathematically mysterious, have a fairly easy time of it. Religion, whether embraced or attacked, is common property; and everybody, from grudge-bearing Joe Public, whose baby was inadvertently dropped into the font by the Vicar, to those sophisticated nineteenth-century secularists who are ever with us, feels entitled to "know better" than the theologian in a way in which they would never dream of "knowing better" than a nuclear physicist or a neurologist. To many, the discipline of Christian Thought (if such it may be called) is redundant; it is partisan; it cannot be pursued objectively; it has no place within the curriculum of higher education.

It is worth reminding ourselves in passing both that this is a relatively recent protest, and that the attitude of some Christians has almost demanded that the protest be lodged. Let us consider each point in turn.

First, for most of the history of Western higher education a Christian context has been assumed. Although, for example, in the earliest Oxford and Cambridge colleges, theology as such was little studied, the Church was nevertheless the gateway to all of the professions; so that a person contemplating a medical or a legal career would first take holy orders.[2] In the sixteenth century Sir Walter Mildmay made no bones about the reasons why he had founded Emmanuel College, Cambridge (1583):

> We have founded the College with the design that it should be, by the grace of God, a seminary of learned men for the supply of the Church, and for the sending forth of as large a number as possible of those who shall instruct the people in the Christian faith.[3]

Such an objective, though it still motivates many theological colleges and private Christian universities to this day, can no longer be said to inspire secular higher education at large. For many, scepticism rules, and increasing confidence in science has, for many, made God increasingly redundant. As early as 1826 we find Lord Brougham and Thomas Campbell establishing their University of London (subsequently University College), with a view to absolving students from the religious tests which were still in force at Oxbridge. That their foundation did not meet with universal approval is clear from the fact that it was branded "the Godless institution," and that three years later the Anglicans responded by opening the rival King's College. Later in the century, during the debate over the question whether (subject to a conscience clause) religious instruction should be given in Manchester's The Owens College (the forerunner of the University in that city), the *Manchester Examiner and Times* asked, "Have the trustees of this noble, because unsectarian, college given in their adhesion to a principle which, if it durst be expressed in words, means really this

— that every extension of secular knowledge is verily an evil, unless counteracted by a proportionable infusion of theological teaching?"[4] So the *modern* question arises, Is there a place for theology, the Queen of the sciences — or even for the more general study of Christian thought — in the secular palaces of twentieth-century higher education?

Leaving blind prejudice on one side, a reply is called for. It must be admitted that although, as I have claimed, the study of Christian Thought offers one route to a liberal education, there is no guarantee that it will be pursued in a liberal manner. The subject itself is littered with party spirit and irrational expostulations, and some of its teachers and students are prone to both. Hence some of the protests against the discipline. In the eighteenth century, for example, one of John Wesley's companions, Walter Sellon, called Augustus Montague Toplady (the author of the hymn, "Rock of ages, cleft for me") "a flaming Calvinist, a Dagon, a Hooter, a Papist, a Socinian, a Mahometan, the greatest Bigot that ever existed, an Atheist." Toplady was, of course, a clergyman of the Church of England, and he could wax pugilistic too. Sellon, he thought, might have bettered himself had he been born two hundred years sooner, for then, instead of being John Wesley's packhorse, he might "as a reward for your meritorious denial of election, have been elected Tub Orator to the Pelagians of Feversham, or Booking."[5] And that was Toplady on a good day! Such unedifying scrapping is generally confined to book reviews in these days.

What is unacceptable in higher education is the peddling of a party line, any criticism of which is rewarded by low marks; and the refusal to consider alternative points of view. Thomas Witherow (1824–1890), Professor of Church History at Magee Presbyterian College, Londonderry, in the middle of the nineteenth century, knew what he expected from theological professors. He looked back upon the eighteenth century, observed the way in which some teachers had turned a number of the Dissenting academies into unorthodox, "Arian" schools, and thundered, "Heresy in the pulpit may slay her thousands, but heresy from the rostrum slays its tens of thousands."[6] Later in the nineteenth century the Scottish theological college professor, A.B. Davidson (1831–1902), found it impossible to distinguish teaching from preaching. Said he, "A Chair is neither a higher nor a lower place than the pulpit, they are the same thing under slightly different aspects...the occupant of a Chair will be successful just so far as he makes his chair a pulpit, and preaches from it."[7] I find Witherow's party-line approach and Davidson's assimilation of preaching to teaching unacceptable — even in a theological college, but still more so in a University. It is, of course, perfectly proper that those who are training for the ministry of a particular church should hear the official teaching of that Church; but to have it forced upon them, or preached in such a way that the professor's convictions alone are heard, is highly dubious practice. It is practice of this kind which prompts some to deny that the discipline of Christian Thought can be pursued with intellectual integrity. (I cannot resist observing in parenthesis that charges of this kind take on a somewhat amusing character when they emanate from dyed-in-the-wool, sectarian empiricist philosophers, monetarist economists, structuralist English experts, Marxist political scientists, or materialistic physicists. Dr. Johnson once described a Member of Parliament as having "a mind as narrow as the neck of a vinegar cruet."[8] True it is that Christianity has no monopoly of such minds.)

Still, I *am* willing to proclaim what I believe if it seems appropriate to do so, and to defend my convictions to the best of my ability. I am also willing to present views opposed to my own with all the grace and zeal I can muster. The pretence of absolute objectivity is among the first deceptions to be exposed by any student worth his salt. Neither should we overlook the danger to which the philosopher F. H. Bradley pointed when he said of someone that his mind is so open that nothing is retained; ideas simply pass through him. But enough of this defensive swashbuckling! Let it be granted, at least for the sake of argument, that Christian thought can be studied with integrity at the University. Let it further be granted that Christian Thought can challenge, and needs to be challenged by those in the University forum who oppose the Christian faith, or who question the validity of its claims, or who embrace other world views.

 II

Implicit in all I have said so far is the conviction that the discipline of Christian Thought is open to Christians and non-Christians alike. But its primary ingredients — the texts to be read, the arguments to be analyzed, the systems to be investigated — are produced by Christians. Just as I can describe, and analyze, and evaluate Buddhist thought but, short of conversion, cannot be a Buddhist thinker, so many may describe, analyze and evaluate Christian thought; But Christians alone can produce it in the original sense. As we have seen, Christian thinking comes in many styles. Our question now is, What counts as honest Christian thinking? What is it for a specimen of Christian thought to have integrity?

The first point to be made is that most Christian thinking does not find its way into courses on Christian Thought. The texts used there are the more or less articulate productions of the relatively few Christians who are given to writing on themes of that kind. We must shun the aristocratic notion that there is a hierarchy of Christian knowledge and experience at whose pinnacle sits the theologian. Despite what I have said about Joe Public's presumption in teaching the theologian his trade, there is a sense in which the *saintly Christian*, however unlettered, can know more than the most sophisticated theologian. (I do not rule out the possibility that a person may at one and the same time be a saintly Christian and a sophisticated theologian — my teacher, T.W. Manson springs to mind.) The fact remains, as the Puritan Stephen Charnock somewhere bluntly put it, "A man may be theologically knowing and spiritually ignorant." The Heidelberg Catechism of 1563 — surely one of the most warmly devotional of all productions of its kind — opens like this:

Question I

What is your only comfort, in life and in death?

Answer

That I belong — body and soul, in life and in death — not to myself, but to my faithful Saviour, Jesus Christ...

Question II

How many things must you know that you may live and die in the blessedness of this comfort?

Answer

Three. First, the greatest of my sin and wretchedness. Second, how I am freed from all my sins and their wretched consequences. Third, what gratitude I owe to God for such redemption.[9]

A person of faith who can make these replies has a knowledge and an experience which may elude the erudite, the more sceptical of whom would do well to heed Paul's warning to the Corinthians: "To shame the wise, God has chosen what the world counts folly (I Cor. 1: 27). It would be rank Pelagianism to suppose that an A+ in Christian Dogmatics admits to heaven, and it is at least conceivable that the eternal destination of some who have achieved that distinction is elsewhere.

I have made this point as strongly as possible because there is no place for scholarly arrogance where the deep things of faith are concerned. But our main concern must be with those who bestow their writings upon us. I wish to suggest that the marks of rounded articulate Christian thought are integrity in relation to the context of the writing, and in relation to the Gospel. I do not mean to say that authors must discuss all of these in relation to every theme on which they write. My point, negatively expressed, is that writers professing a Christian viewpoint should not play fast and loose with the Biblical text; should not act as if they believed that Christianity is to be created *de novo* each new morning by each individual author; should not disregard the context which they seek to address; and should not deny the Gospel. Integrity is required in all of these matters. Shakespeare's Autolycus said, "Though I am not naturally honest, I am sometimes so by chance."[10] Christian thinkers must endeavour to improve upon that.

First, we need integrity *vis à vis* the Bible. There is a widespread consensus throughout the Christian world that, however it may be interpreted, the Bible is the supreme rule of faith and practice. Thus, the sixth of the thirty-nine *Articles* of the

Church of England (1562) declares that "Holy Scripture containeth all things necessary to salvation: so that whatsoever is not read therein, nor may be proved thereby, is not to be required of any man, that it should be believed as an article of the Faith, or be thought requisite or necessary to salvation."[11] The (largely Presbyterian) Westminster Confession of Faith (1643) begins by saying that although God is manifested in creation and providence, these "are not sufficient to give that knowledge of God, and of his will, which is necessary to salvation." Hence, "it pleased the Lord...to commit [the truth] wholly unto writing, which maketh the holy scripture to be most necessary."[12] To these same words the Second London [Baptist] Confession of 1677 prefixes the words, "The Holy Scripture is the only sufficient, certain, and infallible rule of all saving Knowledge, Faith, and Obedience."[13] With slightly different accents the much more recent *Dogmatic Constitution on Divine Revelation* (1965) of the Second Vatican Council makes very much the same point: "Since everything asserted by the inspired writers must be held to be asserted by the Holy Spirit, it follows that the books of Scripture must be acknowledged as teaching firmly, faithfully, and without error that truth which God wanted to put into the sacred writings for the sake of our salvation."[14]

But it is one thing to uphold the Bible as containing what Christians take to be the supreme revelation of God's mind and purposes, it is quite another to decide how best to approach the text. We have to face the fact that the Bible contains many ancient writings, which were brought together over a period of a thousand years. Its world of thought is very different from our own in many respects; its arrangement is not chronological, and is frequently puzzling; it contains a wide variety of material — history, poetry, narrative, letters, gospels — and the identity of most of the writers eludes us. On the other hand, it cannot be denied that the Bible's main message of salvation has come home to millions — as Christians would say, by the Holy Spirit — whose appreciation of the difficulties I have just announced is slight indeed, and they are none the worse for that. What cannot be contested is that whoever approaches the biblical text is engaged in a process of interpretation: it cannot be otherwise. Indeed, the Bible itself is already a collection of interpretations by many writers: interpretations of the significance of past and present events and, supremely, reflections upon the meaning and challenge of the Cross-Resurrection event.

Biblical interpretation can be a hazardous pursuit. William Robertson Smith (1846–1894) was but one of many whose integrity concerning the Bible put him at odds with his church — in his case, the Free Church of Scotland. He was dismissed from his old Testament Chair at Aberdeen in 1881, though he was not deposed from the ministry of the Church. He was by no means an anti-supernaturalist, but he did contend that the Bible *contained* the Word of God, not that its words were identical to the words of God.[15] As compared with some of the German and Dutch Biblical critics of his day, Smith was moderate indeed. In fact, he criticized the liberal theory of the organic development of religion on the ground that it arose from pantheistic presuppositions, and not from critical research.[16] But as far as his Church was concerned, he went too far. The Smith case illustrates the seriousness with which perceived threats to the authority of the Bible are taken in some quarters. It is a discussion which still rages here and there — and not least in the United States.[17]

If I were asked to select one concise statement which affirms my own understanding of the way to approach the Bible with integrity, I should choose a paragraph from the *Declaration of Faith* of the Congregational Church in England and Wales (1967) — one of the most thorough statements of its kind to have been produced during this century. It reads:

> The Bible must be read with full critical attention if the Church is to discern the truth which is binding and not be in bondage to what is not binding; for the Bible is not free from human error and confusion and contradictions. It is a trustworthy means of grace, not in the sense that it is impervious to criticism but in the sense that through its record we are able to know God reliably and trust him confidently. Through the words of the Bible God in Christ speaks directly to believers and bring home to their lives and to the life of the Church the reality of his claims and promises. There are in the Church other means and agencies which serve to bring its life and thought under the Lordship of Christ; but all of them are rooted in God's revelation of himself in the Bible, and by it they are also to be judged.[18]

By this standard, the practice of reading into the Bible what is not there exemplifies a lack of integrity; and how widespread that practice is! Exegesis is our proper business — drawing *from* the text what is there. Eisegesis is the importing *into* the text of what is not there, but what we wish to find there. Instead of standing under the record, so to speak, we seek to control and manipulate it. William Neil once recounted a delightful example of eisegesis perpetrated by a preacher who took as the text of his sermon the words, "Enoch walked with God; and he was not, for God took him." What those words actually mean is that faithful Enoch died. But listen to the preacher: "Brethren, Holy Scripture tells us that Enoch was not. What was he not? I will tell you. He was not an Episcopalian, for he walked and didn't dance. He was not a Baptist, because he walked and didn't swim. He was not a Presbyterian because he walked with God. Hallelujah, brethren, he was a Methodist, for the Lord took him."[19] This is a gross example, of course. But the temptation to view the Bible through our own spectacles is subtle, and some who should know better have succumbed to it. Thus, for example, the Swedish philosophical theologian Anders Jeffner, has lamented the fact that some doctrinal theologians play fast and loose with the exegetical criteria. He cites the authors of an Anglican-Lutheran dialogue report as declaring that baptism in water in the name of the Trinity was instituted by Christ. Dr. Jeffner remarks,

> To start a discussion in this context of the authenticity of this particular word of Christ would have meant lapsing from their role. My impression is that the doctrinal theologian very often forgets the criteria of truth that he uses as an

exegete, attaching a *prima facie* truth to assertions which according to a critical historical study of the text are false.[20]

That is a word in season. Or again, if the Bible is read exclusively through the eyes of those who are properly concerned with the oppression of the poor in our time, other important insights of the Biblical writers may go undetected.[21] Hence the necessity of exegetical integrity. Hence also the practical usefulness of the checks and balances provided by the tradition of faith. We need integrity in relation to that tradition.

The Bible, after all, is the book of the people. Its writers, no less than ourselves, were hampered by finitude and sin. Hence the importance of reading the Bible in the context of the tradition in its past and present expressions. We need to hear what others have made of it. We need to share our insights with them, and to have our prejudices checked by what they have found. If we neglect this catholic community of interpretation, we shall be in danger of elevating our own primary interest or concern into the only acceptable point of departure for the reading of Scripture. If we then proceed to unchurch those who, as far as we are concerned, cannot see the truth because they are not economically oppressed, or women, or blacks, or Barthians, or Thomists, or Oxford dons, we have adopted a posture of gnostic imperialism, and have embraced the sectarian spirit which says, "Only when you see things exactly as I do, will I have fellowship with you." Moreover, those who adopt this stance are really embracing an ahistorical position which in the end amounts to a denial of the providence and guidance of God through the ages, and in contexts other than their own. So to lock ourselves into our own narrow interpretative framework is to deny the possibility of universals in the Gospel; it is to preclude the necessity of ever defending our position, for everyone else cannot but be mistaken; and ultimately, it is to buy immunity from criticism at the high price of incommunicability with anyone else. It is to do in Christian thought what Wittgensteinian "forms of life" have been said to do in philosophy: to cocoon the speaker, and at the same time to render him speechless.

Those who pay no heed to the catholic community of faith — post-Enlightenment individualists all — deny themselves access to any external standards or norms of responsible interpretation.[22] They are the mirror image of those restorationists who think that they can reproduce without alteration the lifestyle, attitudes and church order of the earliest Christians, as if nothing had happened, historically and culturally, in between. It is all a denial of fellowship, of the catholicity and historicity of the Faith, or the providential guidance of God, and of the illumination of the Spirit through the years. It is a stance which calls to mind the two old Yorkshiremen. One said to the other, "Folks is all queer except me and thee — and I'm not so sure about thee!"

What often underlies the positions just described, which seem to me seriously to lack integrity *vis à vis* the community and tradition of faith, is the conviction that our present context not only influences the terms in which we witness, but also provides all the *content* of that witness. Lesslie Newbigin gets the balance right. If we begin from the context, he says, we often proceed

> by identifying a problem or a cluster of problems, and then go on to outline the Christian answer, which takes the form of a programme or project. This problem-programme syndrome is so pervasive that we do not stand back to look at it. If we do so, it is immediately obvious that...we are in the realm of the Law and not of the Gospel. Our Christian contribution to the situation is then to lay a burden on men's conscience...which can spiritually crush them. How much of our Christian talking about the problems of industry, of economic injustice, of racial equality produces only a paralysing sense of guilt and impotence, or else the blind fanaticism of the crusader who can see no moral issue in the world except the one he has chosen to concentrate on.[23]

As I said earlier, there is much Christian thought which does not address contemporary issues. Individual Christian thinkers do not have to do everything all of the time, and it is perfectly proper for them to select their special spheres of interest, whether historical, systematic, philosophical or prophetic. But if Christian thinkers intend to address their contemporaries on the issues of the day, or to advance a Christian view of the world which takes into account the actual situation of those around them, then integrity in relation to the context is indispensable.

The difficulty is that the term "context" is so seldom analyzed, even by those who would wish to be known as contextual theologians. Let us spend a few moments on this slippery concept. No doubt every theology which becomes rooted in a culture, or which responds to a culture, is to that extent contextual. Such contextualizing has a history which goes back right to the earliest days of the Church. Paul at Athens, the Christian Platonists, the Celtic missionaries, Francis of Assisi, Calvin — these and many others sought to contextualize the Gospel. And what else was Barth doing in our own century when, on reading that the majority of his theological teachers had signed a letter in support of the Kaiser's war policy, he made a contextual response in the name of the Word of God as he understood it, and over against what he regarded as bankrupt liberal theology? The same Karl Barth much later wrote, "Jesus Christ never speaks His prophetic Word generally, or in the void, but always specifically in time to different ages;" and he went on to speak of the community's dangerous "inability or unwillingness to rise up, to cast aside its slothful neutrality and truly to follow Him."[24]

Of course, the way in which contextualizing has been undertaken has sometimes given cause for concern. Some have felt that Paul was not conspicuously successful at Athens; the early Fathers and the Christian Platonists could, and sometimes did, blunt the edge of the Gospel.[25] But it is far better to make the attempt and to fail, than not to make the attempt at all. To the great credit of today's contextual theologians, they proclaim a message which goes deeply into the situation of those to whom they speak. Thus, if Gutiérrez has correctly diagnosed the Latin American predicament when he contends that today's crucial theological challenge comes not from non-believers, but from the poor and exploited ones, who are treated as if they were non-persons, then this is something of which contemporary theology must take careful note.[26]

So far, so good: we seem to be in line with Paul Lehmann who defines "contextualism" acceptably as "that way of doing theology which seeks to explore and to exhibit the dialectical relation between the content and the setting of theology."[27] But when I then read Samuel Amirtham's statement that "the test of theology in any context is its faithfulness to the gospel in that context. There is no extra-territorial accountability,"[28] I begin at once to see warning lights. What are the criteria for determining how far a theology is faithful to its context? Who are the best judges of this? And is it really true that there is no extra-territorial accountability? Here we seem to be on the verge of withdrawal from history and tradition, and from the catholic community of interpretation once more.

The context of a contemporary Christian theology is undoubtedly, in one sense, the immediate environment of the theologizing. The Gospel is new, fresh, in every situation. But it is not invented anew in every place. It is given once and for all by God in Christ through the Spirit. Neither is it given to me as if no one else had ever received it before. It is given in and through and to a fellowship. And this fellowship stretches around the world, back into history, and into heaven itself. I am therefore contending that the context of Christian theology is, literally, infinitely broader than our several localities. Indeed, I would suggest that in the deepest sense the context of Christian theologizing is the eternal purpose and action of the triune God, whose Fatherly love has called and justified us, whose Spirit pleads for us, and whose Son vanquished all that could separate us from God's love and peace — which is a summary of Romans 8: 26–39. In a word, integrity to the context must never exclude integrity to that good news, that Gospel, which transcends and judges all our local contexts.

Winston Churchill once remarked of Stanley Baldwin, "It is a fine thing to be honest but it is also very important to be right." I shall argue shortly that I do not believe that Christians can be absolutely sure that they are right in their fundamental claims: we are not as God, and we do have to walk by faith. But if we take Churchill to mean that sincerity is not enough, then what he says is very important. No doubt Hitler was sincere, but Karl Barth and countless others thought that he was very wrong. Because even good people can be sincerely mistaken, I have been at some pains to indicate those factors of the Bible, the Christian community of interpretation, the context of theology broadly conceived, and the overarching Gospel of the grace of God which together constitute the parameters of Christian thinking of integrity.

On the basis of their interaction with these parameters some, but by no means all, Christian thinkers will feel constrained to offer a Christian world-and-life view to their reading public; and with this possibility we come to integrity in the sense of wholeness. For, basing their thought upon a category or categories which seem to them to be important, such thinkers will attempt to share their perspective on life, to tell us "what it all comes to." This is a mission fraught with difficulties and full of challenge.

In the first place, there is the important consideration that Christianity is a Way before it is a system; you cannot encapsulate a Way between the pages of a book — you have to live it. This is to recall the point I am about the believer and the Heidelberg Catechism and I need say no more about it now.

Secondly, there is the fact that we do not always see all that is there to be seen. Sometimes this "not seeing" is wilful and hence blameworthy, sometimes it is not. When, for example, David Lloyd George said of Neville Chamberlain that he saw foreign policy through the wrong end of a municipal drainpipe, the implication was that Chamberlain was both limited and blameworthy: with some expenditure of effort he might have broadened his horizons. But on other occasions our "not seeing" is a product of our being children of our times, and it is then not culpable. Thus, while many would agree that John Wesley possessed considerable religious insight, and that many of his doctrinal emphases live on to this day, the fact remains that if we value our health we will not pay undue attention to his book on *Primitive Physic*. Or again, the memorial stone to Wesley's contemporary John Howard (c. 1726–90) in St. Paul's Cathedral proclaims that "our national prisons and hospitals improved upon the suggestion of his wisdom, bear testimony to the solidity of his judgment, and to the estimation in which he was held in every part of the civilised world." Howard was in advance of his day in his pioneering for prison reform, and the Howard League for Penal Reform, which perpetuates his name, is active to this day. But I cannot help remembering that this same ahead-of-his-time John Howard wrote to his newly-wedded second wife, "My dear, for the prevention of those discords which I have observed to prevail among married people, it is my wish that in case of any disagreement arising between us my will shall prevail." Attitudes change, and I wonder in which respects the pioneers of *our* time will be regarded as backward two centuries hence. But we cannot blame Howard for being a child of his time — nor T.H. Huxley either who, when Darwin hit upon the principle of the survival of the fittest as the clue to evolution exclaimed, "How extremely stupid not to have thought of that!"

But Christians have traditionally posited a further way of "not seeing" or, at least, of seeing through distorting mirrors. They have spoken of our being blinded by sin. They have said that until God removes the scales from our eyes we cannot begin to see straight. Whereas, according to the troubadours of Tin Pan Alley (in this case, Noel

Gay [1938], Ray Noble [1932] and Lorenz Hart [1940]) it is love which makes the world go round; it is the sweetest thing, but it can leave you bewitched, bothered and bewildered; to these Christians it is sin which makes the world groan and travail; it is the most insidious thing, and it leaves you despairing, disreputable and derailed. I believe that this is to be taken seriously but it needs to be understood aright. Older theologians used to speak of total depravity or total corruption — and they often managed to make themselves thoroughly misunderstood. In fact, as John Whale has written,

> Total corruption does not and never did mean that the stream of human history, instead of being crystal clear, is solid mud; but that it is impure, corrupted in every part of its course; that even the purest ideals and the most disinterested achievements of individuals and societies are...tainted by sinful self-interest and pride.[29]

Reinhold Niebuhr agrees, though he prefers to speak of a distortion of our faculties rather than of total depravity;[30] and this line of thought is echoed by Alan Richardson who comments on Genesis 1:26, "The biblical position can best be summarised by saying that the divine image is defaced but not obliterated at the Fall (or by man's sin)."[31] Richardson calls Adam and Eve, Mr. and Mrs. Everyman, for the point of Genesis 3 is that we all shake our puny fists in God's face and say, "We will not have you to reign over us."

Now theologians who take all of this seriously have to pay attention to the noetic effects of sin. To put it crudely, if sin gets everywhere, our minds are not immune from it, and hence our intellect will be adversely affected by it. We will not see as we ought. In particular, our knowledge of God is imperfect, and this not only because we are finite, but because we are naughty. This line is taken strongly, for example, by a Reformed theologian of the seventeenth century, Benedict Pictet (1655–1724), and on this basis he argued the necessity of divine revelation.[32] However, the recognition of human sinfulness should not result in paralysis, intellectual or other. As Martin Luther wrote to his fellow-Reformer Melanchthon, "Be a sinner and sin boldly, but believe and rejoice in Christ, even more boldly, for he is victorious over sin, death and the world."[33] This is, of course, no exhortation to sinful license; rather, here is a realistic statement of the fact that the believer's actions cannot but be tainted by sin, but that nevertheless they are redeemed by Christ's victory.

Thirdly, those would offer a Christian view of the world are challenged from the philosophical direction. Here the point is that the most they can do — and it is a good deal — is to encourage others, by rational argument, to occupy the standpoint which they adopt, and to see how things look from there. Encourage is the operative word, for there are no knock-down arguments here. Although we can, as it were, stand to one side of our ultimate commitment with a view to commending it, explaining what has led us to adopt it, showing why we deem it preferable to other possible stances, we cannot go behind our ultimate commitment to find a criterion with which to evaluate it — for then it would not be ultimate any more. This difficulty applies to the adumbration of any kind of world view, and not to the Christian world view only. As J.S. Bezzant wrote,

> There is not, nor is there ever likely to be, any view of the meaning, purpose, value and destiny of human life, not even the view that it has none, that is not in a greater or less degree founded upon faith, for neither the negative nor the positive belief is demonstrable, i.e. capable of proof. Judgement, whether positive or negative, to be worth consideration, depends upon whether the faith or the refusal of it, has actual and reasonable grounds.[34]

Happily, many philosophers during this century have been able to agree. At the beginning of the century most philosophers seemed content with such ideas as that "to philosophise is to seek an attitude towards the universe as a whole."[35] They would have understood philosophy to be the expression of a person's "deepest and most cherished convictions."[36] They would have urged their colleagues to construct a view of the whole which would both restrain specialists and enlarge their vision.[37] When J.S. MacKenzie said of the recently deceased Henry Jones that "his philosophy was for him a *faith*,"[38] he was being complimentary. A little later, when the icy blasts of positivism would have quenched any such faith, W.G. DeBurgh was earlier than most in recognizing that the scientist, no less than the religious person, is a person committed to certain basic presuppositions.[39] In the positivist's case, the faith is that the universe is of such a kind that certain types of assertion only are verifiable and therefore (by implication) permissible. In the wake of DeBurgh, Dorothy Emmet argued that the philosopher, like the religious person, utilizes the "given" even if he does not sub-scribed to a body of revealed truths;[40] and Alan Richardson reminded us that such a practice is by no means a modern novelty: philosophers have from ancient times selected key ideas — the water of Thales, the atoms of Democritus — to which they have been in some way committed as the basis upon which they have offered their view of the world.[41] As long ago as 1897, R.M. Wenley wrote that "the agnostic adopts his necessary assumptions in the same way as the theist...faith of some sort exercises sway, even although this fact be obscured from many by the resounding conflict concerning its object, content, nature."[42] The importance of some basic commitment was not denied by W.H. Walsh in his more recent re-working of the metaphysical mines;[43] and some who are regarded as exemplars of linguistic analysis have been willing to concede the point too. Thus, to look no further than moral philosophy, P.H. Nowell-Smith wrote that "what sort of principles a man adopts will, in the end, depend on his vision of the Good Life, his conception of the sort of world that he desires, so far as it rests with him, to create."[44] Stephen Toulmin showed how, in ethical discussion, we sometimes come up against "limiting questions," that is to say, we reach a point at which we have to leave the role of advocate and assume that of judge. A decision is to be made, a conviction must be expressed; at which point, if someone continually presses the question, Why do you say that? he is asking a question to which no answer can be given.[45] Finally, R.M. Hare has noted that "*even* our belief in so-called hard facts rests in the end on a faith, a commitment, which is not in or to facts, but in that without which there would not be any facts."[46]

There are many ways of stating the nature of the faith-commitment of Christian thinkers, but one way is to say that they are committed to the Christ of the Gospel, where "Gospel" is shorthand for the unmerited redemptive initiative of God in Christ, whereby fellowship with God, disrupted by sin, becomes possible once more. Such thinkers will seek to ensure that any synoptic view proposed will be compatible with this fundamental commitment. Thus, for example, it is difficult to see how such thinkers could be out-and-out materialists. What the Christian thinker is attempting is a piece of orderly testimony which grows out of a faith commitment. The testimony will be provisional only, and subject to revision. Not all philosophers will like it, and some will not be able to bring themselves to read it. But, no matter how riddled with logical holes his work may be, as John Heywood Thomas wrote, "It is utterly fantastic to imagine that the religious man must await the philosopher's decision before he can believe. The whole point is that he does believe and will go on believing whatever the philosopher says to him."[47] After all, as P.T. Forsyth had earlier said, "We do not review God's claims and then admit Him as we are satisfied...We do not assent and then trust. That would reduce grace to persuasion, and faith to being talked over or argued down."[48]

So far I have said that the activity of adumbrating a Christian view of the world is challenging in that Christianity, being first and foremost a Way, cannot be totally encapsulated in a book; and also because all writers see only part of the picture because they are limited, sinful children of their time. I have also argued that the attempt to present an orderly testimony of the way things seem to be on Christian terms is not an inherently irrational attempt to make — not least because others have their faith-commitments too. But when we come to the manner of proceeding, we are confronted by yet further pitfalls.

In working out their view of the world, Christian thinkers will often, perhaps normally, have some regard to the prevailing intellectual fashions of their day. This is only what we should expect: they have to have some interest in the soil as well as the seed if they will to communicate adequately with their contemporaries. W.H. Moberly saw nothing untoward in the fact that "from St. Paul and the writer of the Fourth Gospel to the framers of the ecumenical creeds, Christian theology was formulated in the language, and in some relation to the problems, of the philosophy of the time."[49] He contended that something of the same kind was needed in the twentieth century, and some thinkers have been more than willing to oblige. Such thinkers fall into a trap, however, if they suppose that they can simply plunder another philosophical "ism" for its terminology and use it without qualification. If they do this they risk the peril of reducing their own content. Let me give an example to show what I mean.

At a time when Christian thinkers were expressing themselves in relation to, and even in terms of, the fashionable philosophical idealism of their day, W.L. Davidson suggested that the terms "God" and "Absolute" are mutually transferrable according to context. He declared that "'God' is the term more properly designative of the Supreme Being when we are viewing Him as known by us or as revealed to us in our personal relations with Him, whereas 'the Absolute' is more strictly applicable at moments when we are specially conscious to ourselves of the fact that God transcends our knowledge of Him..."[50] For a Christian corrective to Davidson, hear James Iverach:

> To speak of the absolute and unconditioned as synonymous with God, is simply to alter the conception of God...the idealist philosophy makes religion to be simply an aspect of itself, and does not leave us with a God into whose fellowship we may enter, in whose service we may find perfect freedom.[51]

Presumably Iverach would grant the psychological difficulty of worshipping a god who was not conceived of as absolute at least in the sense of being supremely — even exclusively — worthy of worship. His point is rather that an undifferentiated absolute will not suffice the Christian. Over against Davidson, Iverach clearly sees that uncritically to adopt a term from absolute idealism may entail leaving most of your Christian content behind. My way of putting the point is to say that if a Christian thinker wishes to utilize terms from elsewhere he must ever remember that he is acting like an anabaptist, not a poacher.[52] Terms are re-baptized when they are transposed from one world view to another. To suppose otherwise is to commit the logical howler of saying that because the same words fall from the lips of Lao Tse and Christ, or because both Davidson and F.H. Bradley use the term Absolute, Christianity equals either Taoism or absolute idealism. Positively put, the point is that in any commerce between one world view and another we are engaged in an analogical procedure, and we have to take seriously J.M. Keynes's distinction between positive and negative analogy. That is to say, we have to note not only the ways in which A is like B, but the ways in which they are unlike.[53] If Christian thinkers fail to remember this, they will be in danger of putting alien shackles upon their message.

 IV

But these practical and philosophical difficulties which attend any attempt to construct a Christian view of the world almost pale into insignificance before the supreme theological challenge: in the last resort the Christian thinker is confronted by the impenetrable mystery of God. To say this is not to seek an escape from hostile criticism: it is to face up to what H.H. Farmer used to call "the 'Godness' of God."

I am the first to admit that some Christian thinkers have resorted too quickly to mystery as a barricade behind which they might hide from sceptical attack. It may even be that some have relished the concoction of mysteries. Thomas Love Peacock evidently thought so, and in his delightfully satirical novel, *Nightmare Abbey*, he makes Mr. Flosky (alias Coleridge) say this: "I pity the man who can see the connection of his own ideas. Still more do I pity him, the connection of whose ideas any other person can see. Sir, the great evil is, that there is too much commonplace light in our moral and political literature; and light is a great enemy to mystery..."[54] Such mystery-mongering is to be shunned: integrity requires it.

The fact nevertheless remains that before the mystery of God all of our Christian thought is weighed and found wanting. We never cease to be creatures; God never ceases to be God. I concur with Stewart Sutherland who writes, "Critical as one is about appeals to 'mystery' in theology, for such can easily pose as form(s) of intellectual escapism, at least such appeals avoid the *hubris* of an epistemologically direct line to either God or the transcendent.[55]

In his autobiography the seventeenth-century Reformed pastor *par excellence*, Richard Baxter, tells us that when he was younger he had "a far higher opinion of learned persons and books than I have now...experience hath constrained me against my will to know that reverend learned men are imperfect, and know but little as well as I, especially those that think themselves the wisest. And the better I am acquainted with them, the more I perceive that we are all yet in the dark."[56] Small wonder that our articulated Christian world views, incomplete as they must always be, and inconsistent as they often are, are provisional and subject to revision. And what a relief that the salvation of no one depends upon his adopting our articulated world view, or even reading it!

Still, it is one thing to have a proper humility before the divine mystery, it is quite another to refuse to love God with all our mind — however partial our insight may be. Accordingly, this series of lectures will continue!

In this first lecture I have attempted to persuade you that the discipline of Christian Thought may be studied with integrity at a secular university; that Christian thinking of integrity operates (with varying emphases) within the parameters of the Bible, the community of faith past and present, the context widely construed to include the action of the triune God, and the over-arching Gospel of God's grace. I have claimed that the attempt to offer, on these bases, a Christian view of the world, that is, to explicate one's faith-commitment in relation to the realms of thought and life, is not an inherently irrational enterprise; but that in view of our finitude and sin, and *vis à vis* the mystery of God, such a statement will be incomplete and provisional. As Anselm saw, it will ever be a case of faith seeking understanding: it is honest to recognize when wholeness eludes us. But if, as Paul said, we are able to see "only puzzling reflections in a mirror" (I Corinthians 13: 12), we can at least look at the glass and believe that what we are seeing are reflections of the truth. If Christian faith brings us even partially to know God, we shall soon realize that to know him is to worship. I therefore end with two lines from the eighteenth-century hymnwriter Isaac Watts. Watts does not discourage the use of reason, but he knows its limits, and bids us sing:

> Where reason fails with all her powers,
> There faith prevails, and love adores.[57]

NOTES

1. Gordon Harland, *Christian Faith and Society* (Calgary: University of Calgary Press, 1988).

2. See e.g. C.E. Mallet, *A History of the University of Oxford* (London: Methuen, 1924), I: 152; A. Mansbridge, *The Older Universities of England* (London: Longmans, 1923), 15–16; H. Rashdall, *Medieval Universities*, eds. F.M. Powicke and A.B. Emden (Oxford: Clarendon Press, 1936), III: 445; Alan P.F. Sell, "The background to the current RE/ME debate in Britain: An historical sketch," *Religious Education* LXVIII (1973): 42–56.

3. Quoted by C.W. Stubbs, *The Story of Cambridge* (London: J.M. Dent, 1905), 307.

4. Quoted by J. Thompson, *The Owens College* (Manchester: J.E. Cornish 1986), 126.

5. A.M. Toplady, *Works* (London: J. Chidley, 1837), 50, 60. See further, Alan P.F. Sell, *The Great Debate. Calvinism, Arminianism and Salvation* (Worthing: H.E. Walter, 1982; Grand Rapids: Baker Book House, 1983), Ch. III.

6. Quoted by W. J. Grier, *The Origin and Witness of the Irish Evangelical Church* (Belfast: Evangelical Bookshop, [1945]), 12.

7. A.B. Davidson, *Charge delivered to the Rev. Alexander Martin at Martin's inauguration as Professor of Apologetics and Pastoral Theology at New College, 20th October 1897* (Edinburgh, 1897), 53, 58. For a recent study of Davidson see Richard Allan Riesen, *Criticism and Faith in Late Victorian Scotland* (Lanham N.Y.: University Press of America, 1985).

8. James Boswell, *The Journal of a Tour to the Hebrides with Samuel Johnson LL.D.*, 1785, Thursday 30 September.

9. *The Heidelberg Catechism* (Philadelphia: United Church Press, 1962), 9, 11.

10. William Shakespeare, *The Winter's Tale*, IV, iii, 734.

11. *Articles agreed upon by the Archbishops and Bishops of both Provinces and the whole Clergy in the Convocation holden at London in the year 1562*, VI.

12. *The Confession of Faith; agreed upon by the Assembly of Divines at Westminster, with the assistance of Commissioners from the Church of Scotland*, 1643, I.

13. *Confession of Faith put forth by the Elders and Brethren of many congregations of Christians (baptized upon Profession of their Faith) in London and the Country*, 1677, I.

14. *"Dogmatic Constitution on Divine Revelation* (1965)," in *The Documents of Vatican II*, ed. Walter M. Abbott, S.J. (New York: Corpus Books, 1966), 111–128.

15. For a recent account of the Smith case see R.A. Riesen, op.cit.

16. See e.g. W.R. Smith, *Lectures and Essays* (London: A. and C. Black, 1912), 360–361. For the general debate see Alan P.F. Sell, *Theology in Turmoil. The Roots, Course and Significance of the Conservative-Liberal Debate in Modern Theology* (Grand Rapids: Baker Book House, 1986), Ch. II.

17. The literature is vast, but see e.g. Harold Lindsell, *The Battle for the Bible* (Grand Rapids: Zondervan, 1976).

18. *A Declaration of Faith* (London: Congregational Church in England and Wales, 1967), 28.

19. William Neil, *A Plain Man Looks at the Bible* (London: Collins Fontana, 1956), 113.

20. A. Jeffner, *Theology and Integration. Four Essays in Philosophical Theology. Acta Universitatis Upsaliensis. Studia Doctrinae Christianae Upsaliensia*, 28 (Stockholm: Almquist & Wiksell International, 1987), 36.

21. For a detailed and sensitive discussion of this point see Gabriel Fackre, *The Christian Story, A Pastoral Systematics. II: Authority* (Grand Rapids: Eerdmans, 1987), Ch. II.

22. See Anthony Thiselton in Roger Lundin, A.C. Thiselton and Clarence Walhout, *The Responsibility of Hermeneutics* (Grand Rapids: Eerdmans, 1985), 110.

23. Lesslie Newbigin, "Context and Conversion," *International Review of Mission*, LXVIII (271, July 1979): 301–312.

24. K. Barth, *Church Dogmatics* IV, 3, 2 (Edinburgh: T. & T. Clark, 1962), 823.

25. See e.g. Alan P.F. Sell, "Theology and the Philosophical Climate: Case Studies from the Second Century A.D.," *Vox Evangelica* XIII (1983): 41–65 and XIV (1984): 53–64; Ibid. "Platonists (ancient and modern) and the Gospel," *The Irish Theological Quarterly* XLIV (1977): 153–174. Sometimes, too, the Church suppressed contextualizers. Thus,

> The early Jesuit missionaries in Asia, associated with the missionary outreach of the Counter-Reformation, gave us a superb example in this matter in the late 1500s and early 1600s before they were suppressed in the infamous controversy of Rites. Thus Matteo Ricci (1552–1610) saw the need to relate his theology to the Confucian context of the contemporary Chinese society. Likewise Robert De Nobili (1577–1656) struggled with the intricacies of Brahmin Hinduism in order to apply his message relevantly to that religious philosophy. He was the first non-Brahmin to see and read the Brahmin Vedic scriptures.

So Martin Goldsmith, "Contextualization of theology," *Themelios* IX (1, September 1983): 18.

26. G. Gutiérrez, *The Power of the Poor in History. Selected Writings* (London: SCM Press, 1983), 92, 193.

27. P. Lehmann in *Prospect for Theology*, ed. F.G. Healey (London: Nisbet, 1966), 131.

28. S. Amirtham, "Theological Education in Europe," excerpts from a lecture, *Ecumenical Press Service*, 86.01.21.

29. J.S. Whale, *Christian Doctrine* (1941; reprint, London: Collins Fontana, 1957), 40.

30. R. Niebuhr, *The Nature and Destiny of Man* (London: Nisbet, 1941), I: 309–10.

31. Alan Richardson, *Genesis I–XI. The Torch Bible Commentaries* (London: SCM Press, 1952), 54.

32. Benedict Pictet, *Theologia Christiana* 1696, I, iii, 2–3.

33. M. Luther, *Works* (Philadelphia: Fortress Press, 1963), XLVIII: 282.

34. In A.R. Vidler et al., *Objections to Christian Belief* (Harmondsworth: Penguin Pelican, 1965), 70.

35. R.F.A. Hoernlé, *Studies in Contemporary Metaphysics* (London: Kegan Paul, 1920), 11.

36. John Watson, *The Philosophical Basis of Religion* (Glasgow: Maclehose, 1907), 1.

37. A.N. Whitehead, *Process and Reality* (New York: Simon & Schuster, 1960), 26.

38. See his critical notice of H. Jones, "A Faith that Enquires," in *Mind* XXXI (1922): 343. For the background to these remarks see Alan P.F. Sell, *The Philosophy of Religion 1875–1980* (London and New York: Croom Helm, 1988), Ch. II.

39. See W.G. DeBurgh, "Logic and Faith," *Philosophy* I (1926): 419–435.

40. D.M. Emmet, *The Nature of Metaphysical Thinking* (London: Macmillan, 1946), 227.

41. A. Richardson, *Christian Apologetics* (London: SCM Press, 1947), 35–36. Cf. J.V. Langmead Casserley, *The Christian in Philosophy* (London: Faber, 1949), 193.

42. R.M. Wenley, *Contemporary Theology and Theism* (Edinburgh: T. & T. Clark, 1897), 130.

43. W.H. Walsh, *Metaphysics* (London: Hutchinson, 1963), 165–166.

44. P.H. Nowell-Smith, *Ethics* (Harmondsworth: Penguin, 1954), 313.

45. S.E. Toulmin, *An Examination of the Place of Reason in Ethics* (Cambridge: Cambridge University Press, 1959), Ch. XIV.

46. R.M. Hare in *Faith and Logic*, ed. B. Mitchell (London: Allen & Unwin, 1957), 192. For some early reflections on this point see Alan P.F. Sell, "Christian ethics and moral philosophy: some reflections on the contemporary situation," *The Scottish Journal of Theology* XVI (1963): 337–351, especially Section III.

47. J. Heywood Thomas, *Subjectivity and Paradox* (Oxford: Blackwell, 1957), 143.

48. P.T. Forsyth, *The Principle of Authority* (1913; reprint, London: Independent Press, 1952), 146.

49. W.H. Moberly, "God and the Absolute," in *Foundations*, ed. B.H. Streeter (London: Macmillan, 1912), 427.

50. W.L. Davidson, *Recent Theistic Discussion* (Edinburgh: T. & T. Clark, 1921), 153.

51. James Iverach, *Theism in the Light of Present Science and Philosophy* (London: Hodder & Stoughton, 1900), 307, 292.

52. See Alan P.F. Sell, "The Peril of Reductionism in Christian Thought," *The Scottish Journal of Theology* XXVII (1974): 48–64; cf. idem., *The Philosophy of Religion 1875–1980*, 28–31.

53. See S.L. Stebbing, *A Modern Introduction to Logic* (London: Methuen, 1930), 250.

54. Thomas Love Peacock, *Headlong Hall and Nightmare Abbey* (London: Oxford University Press, 1929), 173.

55. S.R. Sutherland, *Being and Truth. Essays in Honour of John Macquarrie*, ed. A. Kee and E.T. Long (London: SCM Press, 1986), 126.

56. Richard Baxter, *Autobiography* [i.e. *Reliquiae Baxterianae*, 1696, abridged] (London: J.M. Dent, 1931), 114.

57. From Isaac Watts's hymn, "We [originally 'I'] give immortal praise."

DOCTRINAL INTEGRITY

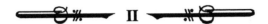

DOCTRINAL INTEGRITY

The Kaz Iwaasa Lecture

Thomas Watson was among nearly two thousand ministers of religion who were ejected from their livings in the Church of England between 1660–1662. They felt that they could not, in conscience, give their "unfeigned assent and consent" to the Book of Common Prayer, the book prescribed by law for use in worship. They could not accept that it was the monarch's prerogative to legislate for the worship and order of Christ's Church. Deprived of his living, Watson continued to preach and teach as he was able, but he died in 1686 — three years before the Toleration Act came into force. Under that Act, Dissenters were given a measure of religious freedom under certain conditions. Six years after Watson's death there appeared the first edition of his *magnum opus, A Body of Practical Divinity* (1692). This work includes his exposition of the *Westminster Shorter Catechism*, on which so many generations of English-speaking Presbyterians cut their devotional and doctrinal teeth. In a "Preliminary Discourse," Watson takes his cue from some words in Paul's letter to the Colossians 1: 23, and argues that Christians need to be settled in the doctrines of the Faith, and that to be settled is to be well-grounded. He pulls no punches: "To be unsettled in religion, argues want of judgment. If their heads were not giddy, men would not reel so fast from one opinion to another. It argues lightness. As feathers will be blown every way, so will feathery Christians."[1] Not surprisingly, he declares that "to preach and not to catechise is to build without foundation."[2]

The practical and devotional worth of Thomas Watson's writings is by no means exhausted, but I cannot now expound him further. I have introduced him simply as an example of a believer in doctrinal integrity — integrity here in the sense of wholeness. Watson believes that the careful study of the Bible yields a system of truth such as is contained in the *Catechism*. The several doctrines of the Christian faith cohere, and together comprise a unity which may be studied systematically.

To all of which divines from all Christian traditions would say Amen! Back in the thirteenth century, for example, we find Thomas Aquinas arguing that because man is directed to a final end which surpasses his reason, "it was necessary for man's salvation that there should be a doctrine revealed by God, besides the philosophical disciplines investigated by human reason."[3] Some sciences, he continues, "proceed from principles known by the natural light of the intellect, such as arithmetic and geometry," whereas "sacred doctrine is a science because it proceeds from principles made known by the light of a higher science, namely, the science of God and the Blessed."[4] For Aquinas, the subject matter of sacred doctrine is God, and God makes himself known in the Scriptures.

Again, in the century following Thomas Watson, and this time from North America, we find Samuel Hopkins (1721–1803) asking, "Is not a System of Divinity as proper and important, as a system of Jurisprudence, Physic, or Natural Philosophy?"[5] — a question he answered with a resounding "Yes!" — and in two volumes. Hopkins's older contemporary, the English Baptist John Gill (1697–1771), he to whom the adjective "redoubtable" is often applied, was in thorough accord. Said he, "Evangelical truths are spread and scattered about in the sacred Scriptures; and to gather them together, and dispose of them in a regular, orderly method, surely cannot be disagreeable; but must be useful, for the more clear and perspicuous understanding them, for the better retaining them in memory, and to show the connexion, harmony and agreement of them."[6] That was precisely the task Gill set himself, though one must confess to a certain sympathy with the historians Bogue and Bennett, who judged that Gill "seems to inquire how much, rather than how well he could write on every subject."[7]

In our own time the late Gordon H. Clark declared, "The whole Gospel is not just a few disjointed truths. It is an ordered and logical system...God does not ramble in his message to us. His thoughts are not desultory and disconnected."[8] But it is one thing to affirm this (and I shall suggest in a moment that it is a hazardous business to make such an affirmation); it is quite another to contend that one has the whole system of Christian truth sewn up once and for all. Some have said precisely that. Hear the American Nathanael Emmons (1745–1840): "The question among Christians is not, who are probably, but who are certainly right, in their belief in the great and fundamental doctrines of the gospel. There is certainty to be obtained in these points; and all who have obtained it, know that those who differ from them in these points are certainly wrong."[9]

Just over a century ago the doughty Irish Presbyterian, Robert Watts, was no less sure that he had come by *the* system of doctrine. He wrote about it with all the enthusiasm — and with something of the literary style — of a soap salesman:

What astronomy is to the progress of our knowledge of God's works in the starry firmament, such is our grand old Calvinistic Theology to the study of His works as they shine forth in the firmament of revelation. There is not a single doctrine of the analogy of the faith that does not shine out with greater splendour when, in accordance with that system, it is set in its own doctrinal constellation, and traced to its fountain-head in the sovereign grace of our Covenant God. It is the only system of Theology that can be called scientific, as it is the only system which humbles man and exalts God. As its essential elements are divinely set in their systematic relations in the sacred Scriptures, it must ever be regarded as the touchstone of all theological speculations, and the guide of all genuine theological progress.[10]

I cannot suppress the feeling that Watts, the dogged controversialist, is here carried off on a wave of lyricism. He knew quite well that there was more than one variety of Calvinism on offer: indeed, he spent much of his time exposing those whom he deemed traitors to the cause. The fact is that under the umbrella of Calvinism have sheltered supralapsarians and infralapsarians, legalists and antinomians, determinists and libertarians, paedo-baptists and believer-baptists, and many more. The development of Calvinism, and especially the question of how far a wedge may be driven between Calvin and his heirs is a topic of lively debate in some quarters to this day.[11]

It was precisely because of the tendency of many to parcel up doctrine once and for all, while at the same time indulging in theological hair-splitting with those whose parcels were of different size and shape, that William Jay lodged his complaint. Jay (1769–1853) ministered for sixty-two years at Argyle Congregational Church, Bath. He informs us that with the Calvinistic scheme of divinity "my principles accorded generally more than with any other,"[12] but he also expostulated:

what a difference must a Christian and a minister feel, between the trammels of some systems of divinity and the advantage of Scripture freedom, the glorious liberty of the sons of God! The one is the horse standing in a street, in harness, feeding indeed, but on the contents of a bag tossed up and down; the other, the same animal, in a large fine meadow, where he lies down in green pastures and feeds beside the still waters.[13]

What are we to make of it all? It seems to me that *the* doctrinal system of integrity — that is to say, the completely whole, copperbottomed system with no loose ends and no unsolved puzzles, exists, if at all, in the mind of God alone. I intend this as a realistic observation — even as a patently obvious one — but not as a sceptical one. The Puritans, among others, never tired of making the point that while we may apprehend God, we shall never comprehend him. With the prophet of Babylonian exile they would have understood God as saying,

> my thoughts are not your thoughts,
> and your ways are not my ways...
> For as the heavens are higher than the earth
> so are my ways higher than your ways
> and my thoughts than your thoughts.[14]

We may well conclude that what some have called the "seamless robe" of Christian doctrine is inevitably somewhat tattered.

But there is no need whatever to fall into the pessimism of saying, "Because we can never achieve complete doctrinal integrity, we may as well give up and sack all the doctrinal theologians." (There may well be grounds for sacking doctrinal theologians, but that is not one of them!) It is, after all, central to any Christian understanding of things that although God is as he is in all his majesty and mystery, he has nevertheless graciously approached us and made himself known to us — and this supremely in Jesus Christ. For this reason Archdeacon Storr declared that "the connection of Christian dogmas with the Person of Jesus Christ is absolutely vital. If we discuss them apart from Him, we are not discussing Christianity."[15] Or, as P.T. Forsyth put it, "Revelation did not come in a statement, but in a person; yet stated it must be...else it could not be spread; for it is not an ineffable, incommunicable mysticism."[16] With James Orr, I believe

> that Christianity is not something utterly formless and vague, but has an ascertainable, statable content, which it is the business of the Church to find out, to declare, to defend, and ever more perfectly to seek to unfold in the connection of its parts, and in relation to advancing knowledge; that this content of truth is not something that can be manipulated into any shape men's fancies please, but something in regard to which we should not despair of being able to arrive at a large measure of agreement...[17]

I may say in passing that I also endorse Orr's footnote of nearly ninety years ago: "I venture to say that what the Church suffers from to-day is not, as so many think, too much theology, but too little theology, of an earnest kind."

To repeat: although doctrinal integrity conceived as the absolute and perfect system will forever elude us, we may nevertheless proceed to the systematic exposition of Christian doctrines. In some circles it will be objected that the time is not ripe for system-building: there is much ground-clearing of an exegetical kind to be done, not to mention all the philosophical problems concerning the criteria for assessing the truth of doctrinal statements. Now while I quite agree that systematicians of integrity will not proceed in ignorance of the exegetes and philosophers, the posture of waiting until all the ground is cleared may simply indicate a failure of nerve if not of faith.

If we are to proceed, let us proceed honestly. But what does that mean? First, we must admit that our attempt to state Christian doctrine in a systematic way and in sequence involves work of selection and editing, and that this task is inherently judgmental. *We* are deciding what we will pay attention to, what is important, what to include, what to exclude. That done, we then interpret what we have, and recommend the way in which our findings are to be understood. Hence the variations of emphasis, and even the contradictions, between the many doctrinal systems which have been offered down the ages. Back in the eighteenth century, and before the impact of modern biblical criticism, John Gill understood the point well. He wrote, "a Sabellian or a Unitarian and a Trinitarian, will neither of them scruple to say in Scripture-terms what Christ says of himself and his Father, *I and my Father are one*; and yet the former holds that they are one in person or but one person; whereas the latter affirms that they are one in nature and essence, but two distinct persons; and surely it must be lawful so to express himself, if this is the real sentiment of his mind."[18] Let it not be forgotten that the New Testament itself is already a work of interpretation. Paul does not express himself on the Christ or on the atonement in exactly the same terms as the writers of John's gospel or the letter to the Hebrews.

Secondly, honesty prompts the recognition that although doctrinal systems purport to be dealing with eternal truth, they are at the same time inescapably influenced by their times: they have to be if they are to address their times; and no religion which claims a revelation in history can with impunity seek to avoid the relativities of history. Thus there is much to be said for James Orr's position in his book *The Progress of Dogma* [1901], from which I quoted earlier. Orr detects an emphasis upon apologetics — the vindication of Christianity over against paganism — in the first two centuries of the Christian era. He finds a lively concern for the doctrine of God conceived as Trinity in the third and fourth centuries, and a detailed consideration of the doctrine of man in the fifth. At the Reformation the doctrines of justification and sanctification come promptly into view, while eschatology is a primary interest of the nineteenth century. As if by Providence, he suggests, these doctrinal developments follow one classical pattern of systematic doctrinal statement.[19] As I said, there is much to be said for Orr's detection of differing doctrinal emphases at different periods — Christians were responding to their intellectual environments, and the challenges to the Faith were by no means identical in each successive age. But I am not so sure that the chronology follows the classical systematic pattern as closely as he would like. It is interesting, for example, that he omits a period of emphasis upon the doctrine of the Church. It may be that in the future that will be seen to have been the predominant interest of our own century with all its ecumenical activity; but in that case the parallel with classical systems would be broken, for ecclesiology would then come after eschatology, the doctrines concerning last things: heaven, hell, death and judgment.

Thirdly, precisely because of the differing emphases at different times, we may detect differing gaps at different times. Interest and enthusiasm seem to be consumed in one direction at the expense of other directions. Thus, when the so-called Apostles'

Creed was devised the current heresy to be countered was docetism — the idea that Jesus was not really a man, he simply seemed to be such. The Creed counters with blunt affirmations designed to root Jesus the man in history: born of the Virgin Mary; suffered under Pontius Pilate; crucified; died; buried. But, as has often been pointed out, as a rounded statement of the gospel the Creed hardly succeeds. If we say, with Luther, that the doctrine of justification by grace through faith is the article by which the Church stands or falls, we shall look in vain for that article in the Apostles' Creed. Or, as P.T. Forsyth remarked, "The doctrine of Redemption is signally absent from the creeds, yet the Church has a more direct connection with Redemption than with Incarnation. Only by experience of Redemption has it a religious knowledge of what Incarnation means."[20] To give one more illustration: if we examine the classical confessions of faith and catechisms of the Reformed churches we find that they say relatively little about death, judgment, heaven and hell (topics on which the medieval Franciscan friar, Richard of Paris, preached on ten consecutive days for seven hours per day!). The First Helvetic Confession of 1536 devotes two sentences to these doctrines, and three paragraphs to the temporal government. The Belgic Confession of 1561 gives eschatology one out of thirty-seven articles, of which nine concern the Church and the sacraments. And when Thomas Watson expounded the Westminster Shorter Catechism he devoted seventy-four pages to the application of redemption, but only twenty-six to eschatology. How so? Among plausible reasons suggested are that because of their strong doctrine of the perseverance of the saints — that is, the idea that Christians, the elect, will be kept by God eternally — they had little need to speculate upon the last things: all would be well. Negatively, there were so many wild millenarian enthusiasts around that the more sedate Reformed Christians wished to distance themselves from such a rabble. Whatever the reasons, the lack of eschatological emphasis is plain for all to see.

The inescapable conclusion is that because we shall never achieve a perfect system of doctrine; because system-building is fallible, human, interpretative work; and because historical exigencies prompt us to see some things clearly and other things less clearly, or not at all, it ill behooves a Christian theologian to say, or behave as if, the acceptance of his or her system were the criterion of a true believer. Such arrogance would be quite preposterous, though at times — and for all they have thundered about salvation by grace, some have given the impression that salvation is by the work of assenting to a particular "plan of salvation" — namely theirs! The distinguished Scottish theologian, H.R. Mackintosh, knew better: "Theologies from the first have perished; they wax old as doth a garment; as a vesture Time folds them up, and lays them down. Nothing save the Gospel is abiding, and its years shall not fail."[21]

After all — and to end this section with a delightful piece of godly doggerel from the eighteenth-century hymn writer Joseph Hart:

No big words of ready talkers,
No dry doctrine will suffice.

Broken hearts, and humble walkers,
These are dear in Jesus' eyes;
Tinkling sounds of disputation
Naked knowledge, all are vain;
Ev'ry soul that gains salvation
Must and shall be born again.[22]

 II

The crucial importance of regeneration notwithstanding, the "tinkling sounds of disputation" are never silent among Christians, and the tinkling is seldom louder than when what are taken to be vital doctrines are at stake. Granted that we shall never achieve a doctrinal system with no rough edges at all, it does seem to be the case that one doctrine rolls into another, and that from whichever one you begin you have, in the end, to talk about all the others as well. Thus, for example, Christians say that they believe in God. But what sort of God? Well, he has made himself known in Jesus. But in what ways? Well, as a Father who loves us so much that he sent his Son to live and die and rise again for us. But how does this make any difference to us? Well, by his Holy Spirit, and through the preaching of the good news, God calls us into his family, the Church. Is that all? No; for the new life he gives us cannot be destroyed by death, but is eternal in scope.

From that very crude and brisk recitation you can see how one doctrine leads into, and depends upon, another. Physically, we cannot say everything all at once, but nevertheless there is a coherent, widely-accepted core of Christian doctrine, the various parts of which need to be held together. We may not have an absolutely "seamless robe" of doctrinal statement, but we do have more than a heap of miscellaneous remnants.

On this basis I now wish to illustrate the necessity of holding doctrines together if we are not to skew theology. Many examples could be given, but I wish to select two doctrines which are central to Christianity on any reckoning: the doctrines of the person and work of Christ. Or, to give them their more technical titles, Christology (who Christ is), and soteriology (Christ's saving work). My thesis is that these two doctrines need to be held together: indeed, that the most hopeful approach to Christology, the doctrine of the person of Christ, is via soteriology, the doctrine concerning his saving work.

I emphasize at the outset that of course Jesus can only do what he does because he is who he is. In logic and in fact McLeod Campbell was right when he said "the faith of the atonement presupposes the faith of the incarnation."[23] But if we would really begin to see who he is, we must appreciate what he has done. This, after all, is how the early Christians came by their understanding of the Christ. They did not proceed from discussions of the person of Christ to the question of his saving acts. Rather, after what he had done — supremely in the Cross-resurrection event — they began to realize who he was, and to call him Lord, the very word which had traditionally been reserved for God alone. The order of their experience was not, This is who he is, now what can he do? but This is what he has done, who must he be?

Not all theologians have given due weight to this insight during the past two hundred years, and the result has been some unbalanced doctrinal teaching. Let us see how this has come about. I shall first offer a brief sketch of the intellectual climate which helped to foster the distortion, and then give three examples of the lack of balance which I detect.

As compared with eighteenth-century rationalism, and certainly as against the increasingly moribund deism of that century which tended to make God remote from his world and the people in it, the nineteenth century sounds a much more hopeful note. As revolutionary political humanity was beginning to come into its own in France and elsewhere, so in theology the upsurge of emphasis upon the human was no less significant. In the theological realm Schleiermacher (1768–1834) played a key role. For him, Jesus is the supremely God-conscious man; the one in whom our creation is completed. This claim is established, thinks Schleiermacher, not because of a Biblical account of a Virgin Birth, or because of the miracle of the resurrection, but because we have experienced God's saving power in Jesus. On the basis of this experience we may well wish to make claims concerning Christ's divinity, but first comes human experience. Consistent with the mood of the Romantic age, the older arguments for Christianity which relied upon the rational appraisal of external evidences of God's existence drawn from the order of nature, for example, or which regarded the miracles of Jesus as *evidence* of his divinity, were gradually replaced by this psychological-anthropological approach.

Coleridge (1772–1834) was among Englishmen profoundly influenced by this current of thought; in America, William Ellery Channing (1780–1842) was but one of many who asserted the dignity of humanity over what he took to be Calvinism's denigration of humanity; and his fellow Unitarian, the Englishman James Martineau (1805–1900), contended that the seat of authority in religion was not the Bible, the Church or Tradition, but the conscience.

This inward, immanentist thrust — much indebted as some of it was to the German philosopher Hegel and some of his followers — was construed by many theologians as bringing God closer than before. God was proclaimed as active in the universe and in human life, and some managed to interpret the findings of evolutionary science as evidence of, or at least as consistent with, this involvement of God in all things. The God of the human conscience was also the God of the created order, and he was working within both, ever moving all things towards his final consummation. Not surprisingly, development is a key concept in much late nineteenth-century thought, theological and other.

The more distinctly doctrinal contribution which came with the revival of interest in the early Fathers of the Church — especially the Greek Fathers — reinforced the tendency to regard God as close, and God and humanity as united in the Christ who became incarnate. This line of approach, already evident in the writings of the Anglican F.D. Maurice (1805–72) was reinforced by the rediscovery of the Classics at Oxford under the inspiration of Benjamin Jowett around the middle of the century. Anglican theology in particular paid increasing attention to the Incarnation motif.

Even from this rapid survey of a mass of complex subjects,[24] we can detect certain welcome correctives to the received position of much Protestant theology. That theology was bluntly described by Benjamin Jowett thus: "God is represented as angry with us for what we never did; He is ready to inflict disproportionate punishment on us for what we are; He is satisfied by the sufferings of His Son in our stead."[25] There is an element of caricature here, but there is no smoke without fire. Some had proclaimed a so-called plan of salvation which seemed to take its point of departure from the sin of humanity rather than from the grace of God. We were miserable, hope-less, utterly doomed; God was holy, righteous, angry; and the Atonement came to be seen as the focal point in the buying off of this wrathful deity. Against all such theories Maurice rightly protested that they made sinful humanity and not the God of all grace the foundation of Christian theology.[26] The strong emphasis upon God's righteous *will* (sometimes referred to as his *inscrutable* will — and how much some of them thought they knew about that!) goes right back, on both Protestant and Catholic sides, to Augustine. If will tended to replace grace, so sovereignty tended (despite the Gospels) to be divorced from Fatherhood.[27] How could we be sure that such a God really loved us?

In fact, it was precisely McLeod Campbell's dismay at the pastoral results of the received system of doctrine that prompted him to turn the system on its head. His parishioners were joyless, forever indulging in introspection to see if they had the signs of regeneration within their souls, desperately anxious to believe that they had not committed the unpardonable sin, and that salvation might, after all, be for them. All of this led Campbell to make God's love in Christ's Incarnation and Atonement the first word of his preaching. It was a most welcome and healthy emphasis, though for his pains Campbell was subsequently deposed from the ministry of the Church of Scotland.[28]

Like Maurice, Campbell was concerned to see the whole of Jesus's life and ministry — and not only his death — as having to do with God's saving purpose. At this point he was in fact recovering an insight of Calvin which had so often been forgotten by those of the Calvinist tradition; for Calvin had taught that the efficacy of Christ's work was not limited to his death, but concerned "the whole course of his obedience."[29] The fresh emphasis upon this truth in the nineteenth century was a further benefit which flows down to us from that time. I believe that we can safely say that the life of Jesus, and not only his death, raises the Christological question. To give one example: some people say, "We have no time for this heavy doctrinal stuff about 'very God and very man' — but we do like the Sermon on the Mount." Now, quite apart from the fact that the teaching in the Sermon on the Mount reveals, if anything does, our need of a Saviour and not just of one more moral teacher, for we just cannot begin to live by that teaching unaided, how closely have the challengers really read the Sermon? Listen to R.W. Dale on this point:

> Who is this that places persecution for his sake side by side with persecution for righteousness's sake, and declares that whether men suffer for loyalty to him or for loyalty to righteousness they are to receive their reward in the divine Kingdom? Who is it that places his own authority side by side with the authority of God...Who is it that in that sermon assumes the awful authority of pronouncing final judgment on men?...Who is he? That question cannot be silenced when words like these have once been spoken.[30]

As one who is pleading for doctrinal integrity — for the holding together of things which belong together — I shall not side with any who wish to fasten exclusively upon the death of Christ, as if his life were of no account. His whole incarnate life matters, as does his continuing influence and presence by the Holy Spirit; and all of it poses the Christological question, Who is he?

The final benefit of the fresh emphasis in the nineteenth century upon the Incarnation to which I would draw your attention is the justification and motivation it provided for concerted Christian socio-political witness and service. I cannot take time to demonstrate the point in detail here; but the Christian Socialism of Charles Kingsley comes to mind as an obvious example of this concern, as does the philanthropic activity of the evangelicals of the Clapham Sect. And why do so many — even those who would define themselves as irreligious — respect so highly the Salvation Army (that characteristically nineteenth-century creation) if not for its most practical concern for all sorts and conditions of people? As the Anglican scholar B.F. Westcott wrote, "The Incarnation binds all action, all experience, all creation to God; and supplies at once the motive and the power of service."[31] I would add that since, in Christ, a *people* is bound to God, the protest against atomistic individualism, and the importance of the Church as a community are implicitly underscored.

So much for the gains. But I do detect in some writers a swing of the pendulum away from excessive emphasis upon the Atonement to excessive emphasis upon the Incarnation. So to my three examples.

First, let us examine the controversy between F.D. Maurice, to whom I have already referred with approval, and the Scottish theologian Robert Smith Candlish (1806–73).[32] Maurice strongly advances the view that humanity is already redeemed in Christ, who is the root of the new humanity. This is why he has, as we saw, little patience with that theology which focuses in the first place upon sin. There is no good news in that, he thinks. On the contrary, he writes, "It is the effect of sin to make us look upon ourselves as the centres of the universe; and then to look upon the perverse and miserable accidents of our condition as determining what we ourselves are; so all the manifestations of God are treated as if they were appropriate to those accidents.[33] Very well; but how, then, is the supreme work of Christ, the atoning sacrifice, to be regarded? In a characteristic passage Maurice writes,

> supposing the Father's will to be a will to all good, the Son of God, being one with Him, and Lord of man, to obey and fulfil in our flesh that will by entering into the lowest condition into which men had fallen through their sin; — supposing this Man to be, for this reason, an object of continual complacency to His Father, and that complacency to be fully drawn by the Death of the Cross; is not this, in the highest sense, Atonement? Is not the true, sinless root of Humanity revealed; is not God in Him reconciled to man?...Is not the Cross the meeting point between man and man, between man and God?[34]

Now it must be said that Maurice is not always the clearest of expositors. Indeed, he said of himself, "I have laid a great many addled eggs in my time."[35] It does, however, seem quite clear that he is advancing something stronger than a subjective theory of the atonement which would turn Christ's sacrifice simply into a God-given, exemplary visual aid designed to promote some kind of effect in us. For Maurice Christ is representative Man who, in his self-offering to God, draws all humanity with him, and draws out the Father's complacency towards us all. This, at least, was done at the Cross; and in the implication that God was pleased with what was done there is an objective element. Maurice can thus rightly call the Atonement, in his sense, a transaction.[36]

But is enough done here? Robert Mackintosh thought not: "Maurice," he declared, "with his Alexandrian preoccupations, hardly knows what to say about the death on Calvary."[37] Here Mackintosh is directly in the line of Candlish who, in 1854, had published his full-scale *Examination of Mr. Maurice's Essays*. Candlish poses the question at issue thus: "Does God deal judicially with his intelligent creatures? Does he try and judge, to the effect of acquitting or condemning, the persons of men — you, my brother, personally, and me?"[38] Significantly, while Candlish notes Maurice's indebtedness to Coleridge, he remarks that Maurice "does not appear to have pushed his inquiries so far as Coleridge did, into man's sinful nature and the Almighty's moral government...there is an entire omission of the fact of guilt, as a real fact in our history, and a fact with which a righteous God must deal."[39] Candlish therefore feels that to Maurice, the Incarnation is not part of a saving process which God is working out; "It is not...essential to man's redemption. It is rather the full and complete exhibition of it."[40] Similarly, Candlish continues, to Maurice the Atonement merely demonstrates God's dislike of the unlovely; there is no "actual removal from us of the wrath and condemnation under which we personally were before."[41] In a nutshell, as far as Candlish can see, there is, in Maurice's theory, "a careful and consistent disavowal of anything really being done by God."[42] I have already given my verdict that there is a trace of objectivity in Maurice's position; but where according to Candlish, Maurice's teaching leaves us with the sympathy of God, Candlish thinks that nothing short of a substitutionary death on the Cross will suffice if God's righteousness is to be satisfied.[43]

Candlish is very much at pains to deny the caricatures which some were painting of his own position. He declares:

> We do not hold that Christ in any sense changed the will of the Father. We do not hold that the Atonement moved the Father to love the world, but that the Father so loved the world as to provide the Atonement...we believe that because Christ is the actual representative of men, he is on that very account qualified to be their substitute...We believe that [the death of Christ] is not a sacrifice of man to God, but a sacrifice for man...[by] the man Christ Jesus, who gave himself a ransom for all.[44]

In a subsequently-published *Letter* Candlish returned to his charge: "The Atonement is in [Mr. Maurice's] teaching stripped of every vestige of the idea of a real satisfaction to Divine justice, and a real expiation of human guilt."[45]

To express my interim umpire's verdict: I can well understand that Maurice would feel repelled by some of the ways in which the penal substitutionary theory of the Atonement was handled in his time: the Father is not crudely to be set over against the Son. On the other hand, I do not think that Maurice takes the full measure of sin as an affront to the holy love of a righteous God. He evaporates the judicial element, and I cannot entirely endorse the verdict of B.M.G. Reardon that Candlish's response to Maurice, when set alongside Maurice's breadth of vision concerning the union of the creation and atonement motifs in the Incarnate Christ, now seems "narrow and antiquated."[46] Narrow, perhaps, but not antiquated.

IV

For our second example we cross the water to Pennsylvania, where we find the development, contemporary with F.D. Maurice, of the Mercersburg theology. This theology took its name from the German Reformed seminary which, together with Marshall College, was the place of its birth.[47] The first phase of the movement was philosophical. The pioneer of this aspect was the first President of Marshall College, F.A. Rauch (1806–41), whose characteristically nineteenth-century advocacy of a principle immanent in all things, proved a useful foundation upon which his theological colleagues could build their Christocentric, incarnational doctrines. These theologians included Philip Schaff (1819–93),[48] the eminent historian of Christian doctrine, whose friendship with F.D. Maurice was significant; and John Williamson Nevin (1803–86), the former Presbyterian, who became the driving theological force in the Mercersburg movement.

The Mercersburg theology is a fascinating subject of study, and from it insights are being mined to this day. Strongly Christocentric and incarnational, its exponents had a deep commitment to the Church conceived as Christ's mystical body, and hence, as catholic. They had a corresponding hatred of sectarianism. Their respect for the Church of the ages contributed to their appeals for liturgical revision within the German Reformed Church — all of which was too much for some of their co-religionists to stomach. There were numerous controversies. Nevin was accused of Romanizing tendencies, though in fact he castigated Anglo-Catholicism for its inconsistency, and regarded the Roman papal and hierarchical attitudes with grave distaste. A few left the German Reformed Church for domiciles deemed more catholic;[49] Ursinus College was founded by Nevin's liturgical opponents;[50] and its first President was his erstwhile defender turned antagonist, J.H.A. Bomberger (1817–90).[51] There were no major secessions, however, and in 1881 the report of the Church's Peace Commission was adopted, all sides by then having learned something.

It was Bomberger who took up the cudgels against Nevin over the question of the atonement. Nevin's position was quite clear: "The mediation of Christ, we say, holds primarily and fundamentally in the constitution of his person. His Incarnation is not to be regarded as a device *in order* to his mediation...it is itself the Mediatorial Fact..."[52] Again, "the whole being of Christianity, the new world of grace in which only the world of nature itself becomes complete, is rooted...in the Incarnation of the...Divine Logos, whereby He became man for us men and for our salvation."[53] It is quite true, Nevin later says, the "the Saviour must come into the world, before He could die in the world,"[54] but the Incarnation "is not to be viewed as a mere outward device for making the Atonement possible...Here precisely is the fallacy and falsehood of the view I am now opposing, that it resolves the whole Gospel into the atonement, and makes the death of Christ to be the ultimate and only end of His coming into the world."[55] In *The Mystical Presence* Nevin applied his teaching to ourselves:

> The atonement as a foreign work, could not be made to reach us in the way of a true salvation. Only as it may be considered *immanent* in our nature itself, can it be imputed to us as ours, and so become available in us for its own ends...When Christ died and rose, humanity died and rose at the same time

in his person; not figuratively, but truly; just as it had fallen before in the person of Adam.[56]

All of which seemed to make our salvation too inevitable and automatic, as far as Bomberger was concerned. The rupture and discontinuity of sin was not sufficiently allowed for; and there was a corresponding weakness as to the radical nature of the remedy required. The German theologian, I.A. Dorner, agreed: for Nevin, he wrote, "Christ is the self-revealing centre for Christianity; *and here where it should be named, no mention is made of the necessity of conversion, as a proper condition and basis of true knowledge, as though every man in Christendom understood of himself that Christ was this centre.*"[57] In comparing the Mercersburg with the Reformed theology, Bomberger characterized the crux of the matter thus:

> Reformed theology teaches, that the Word became flesh in order to redeem lost man from the punishment of sin, by Christ enduring that punishment, in His Human nature, in man's stead; and to restore man to the favour of God, and to newness of life, through the Holy Spirit.

> Mercersburg maintains the Word became flesh, *not* so much to make atonement for the sin of the world, by offering Himself as an expiatory sacrifice, *but* that by joining Himself to the race, He might infuse into mankind the very substance of His own divine-human or theanthropic life, and in this way (pantheistically) save the race.[58]

There the lines are clearly drawn.

In a Memorial Discourse following Bomberger's death, F.F. Bahner wrote, "His doctrinal system was intensely Pauline, and he had little sympathy with that type of theological dogma and life which may be denominated Johannean."[59] We may add that Bomberger was not often in the spirit of the letter to the Hebrews. Nevertheless, (and despite the fact that Nevin repudiated Bomberger's interpretation of Mercersburg theology) in sounding a warning note against "immanent-automaticism" in the matter of our salvation, I believe that Bomberger did well.

V

For our third illustration we move back to England, and forward one century. En route, however, we may pause to note the opinion of the Anglican Handley G.C. Moule, which he expressed in a letter written to Robertson Nicoll on 19 January 1898. He refers to Nicoll's latest book, and says, "very specially, I have again and again given thanks for your strong and reasoned witness to exactly that range of truth — the truth of guilt and of Cross-won remission and acceptance...which is now so widely ignored if not rejected — and the absence of which seems always to me to bring a long and dreary falsetto into the whole music of theology."[60] I suspect that Moule *redivivus* would have detected a "long and dreary falsetto" in the volume of essays entitled *The Myth of God Incarnate* (1977) — our third illustration.

Where Maurice and the Mercersburg theologians were eager to emphasize the Incarnation and the union of all things in Christ, the mythographers, as they have come to be called, contend that incarnational language is but a "mythological or poetic way of expressing [the] significance [of Jesus] for us"[61] One of them, Maurice Wiles, poses the question: "Are we sure that the concept of an incarnate being, one who is both fully God and fully man, is after all an intelligible concept?"[62]

The practical consequences of the traditional doctrine of Incarnation are among the perfectly proper concerns of the mythographers. In particular, they are exercised by the implications of that doctrine for our relations with people of other faiths.[63] Are Christians damagingly exclusivist in the claims they make for Christ? This question raises that of the nature, objectives and methods of Christian mission — and to that confused and confusing territory I shall return in my penultimate lecture.

All I wish to do now is to offer some evidence for my feeling that the non-exclusivist motive which operates in this collection of essays leads to weakness on the atonement doctrine, and hence to a weakness in Christology. The mythographers, given their concerns, are almost bound to have difficulties with the so-called scandal of particularity: why did God act here, and not there? Their response seems to have been not to dwell over much on the *act* of God in history, but rather to transpose the atonement into a significant story concerning what God is ever doing on behalf of us all. As before, it is the transcendent holiness of God and the exceeding sinfulness of sin which are at risk.[64]

Of all the mythographers, Frances Young comes closest to taking this point. She, like her fellow-writer John Hick,[65] well understands the order of events by which the early Christians came by their Christological claims:

The early Christians were searching for categories which could adequately express their sense of salvation in [Jesus]...It was the sense that they had found what they were looking for in Jesus that started the whole christological ball rolling — in other words, christological formulations derive from a sense of having experienced God's promised salvation (however interpreted) in and through Jesus Christ.[66]

It is good to have this confirmation of my own view from a patristic scholar. Dr. Young further agrees that "in any attempt to rethink christological belief, the primacy of soteriology must be recognized."[67] But then she spoils it. She immediately defines soteriology as "this sense that the story of Jesus Christ provides the key to life, the answer to man's moral idealism, and above all, a revelation of divine involvement in the suffering and evil of the world, has been mediated to us through the faith of generations committed to the church, and through the witness of the New Testament."[68] I can almost hear Candlish and Bomberger thundering, "but we are not here dealing with a story that provides the key to life, but with an action that offers life through death!"

In fairness to Dr. Young, she does proceed to say

Salvation and atonement are the core of the Christian message...It is only because I can see God entering the darkness of human suffering and evil in his creation, recognizing it for what it really is, meeting it and conquering it, that I can accept a religious view of the world...Faith demands a doctrine of atonement, and atonement means a conviction that God has somehow dealt with evil...[69]

I would add in passing that Atonement means not our conviction that God has somehow done something, but the fact that he has. But my main point here is that the implications of this soteriology are not carried forward into Dr. Young's Christology, and still less into that of her colleagues. If all that she says is true, who must he be?

John Hick appears to expect less of an Atonement than Frances Young. In the follow-up volume to the *Myth* he rightly declares that "the idea of the cross transforming God's own nature and state is not theologically viable." Candlish and Bomberger say Amen! God is ever gracious, and does not require to be turned from hatred to benevolence by Christ's sacrifice. On the contrary, he lovingly provides, is in and receives, the sacrifice. It is, as Paul said, God in Christ reconciling the world to himself.[70] But Dr. Hick would not wish such texts to be construed in an exclusivist manner. He asks,

May we not say that although the cross, and the incarnation as a whole, whilst not exclusively constituting God's co-suffering with humanity, nevertheless *reveals* that co-suffering and so enables us to believe it? Could it not be that God has always suffered with the suffering of his creatures, and always been hurt by their sins, but that the cross of Christ makes this divine suffering visible as an event in human history?[71]

It may all be said; it must all be said; but some feel that there is more to be said if the Cross is more than a visual aid. If that is the only way it is regarded, will not a reduced soteriology, and hence a reduced Christology, be the inevitable consequence? Is God, at the Cross, merely showing us something about himself as fellow-sufferer, or is he vanquishing once and for all everything that would keep us apart from him? The crucial trio of questions is: What needed to be done in order to make our redemption possible? What has been done? Who alone could do it?

Concerning this last question, although the mythographers express reservations concerning the classical two-nature doctrine of the person of Christ, it would be quite wrong to charge them with setting out to disturb the faithful by the concoction of theological novelties. They justifiably declare that "there is nothing new in the main theme of this book, and we make no pretence to originality."[72] Indeed, when Frances Young says that "each man is potentially 'God incarnate,' "[73] she does not seem very far removed from the Unitarian James Martineau who, one hundred years ago, asserted that "the Incarnation is true, not of Christ exclusively, but of Man universally, and God everlastingly."[74] At least one present-day Unitarian theologian has detected the appropriation of Unitarian doctrine by the mythographers and others.[75]

The mythographers' desire to liberate Christology from a narrowness which would seek to localize and constrict the saving work of the eternal Logos, who is savingly competent beyond and despite Christian boundaries, is worthy indeed. But it does seem, in their case, to turn upon soteriological vagueness. Thus, for example, Maurice Wiles thinks it may be claimed that "it is supremely through Jesus that the self-giving love of God is most fully expressed and men can be caught up into the fullest response to him. For Jesus was not merely a teacher about God; the power of God was set at work in the world in a new way through his life, ministry, death and resurrection..."[76] This is a little vague. In what way, or to what end was the power of God set at work in the world in a new way? Traditional Christianity has an answer in terms of God's holiness and grace, and our sin and need. We find little consideration of this in the *Myth*. If our predicament is less grave than we thought, no doubt a lesser Christ will suffice.[77]

The nub of the matter is that Jesus does not need to be very God and very Man in order to do what most of the mythographers deem to be necessary to salvation. They appear to be firmly in the line of Benjamin Jowett who, in the middle of the last century, pronounced that "the only sacrifice, atonement, or satisfaction, with which Christ has to do, is a moral and spiritual one; not the pouring out of blood upon the earth, but the living sacrifice 'to do thy will, O God'; in which the believer has part as well as his Lord."[78] Halfway between Jowett and ourselves, P.T. Forsyth put his finger on the weakness of that approach: "The juristic aspect," he wrote, "is a real element in Christ's death...The chief defect of the great revolution which began in Schleiermacher and ended in Ritschl has been that it allowed no place to that side of Christ's work."[79]

VI

It is now time to gather up the threads of my argument. I have suggested that a theological system of absolute integrity, in the sense of wholeness or completeness, must forever elude us, both because of who we are, and because of who God is. We should not, on this account, refrain from attempting systematic statement of Christian doctrine if that is our calling, though we must recognize that our systems are necessarily imperfect, provisional and open to revision. In proposing any doctrinal system, integrity in the sense of honesty will prompt us to give due weight to the several Christian doctrines which have been hammered out over the centuries.

I illustrated my case by reference to the need to balance what we say about the Incarnation of Christ with what we say about the Atonement. The question posed by Maurice and Nevin was whether their emphasis upon the Incarnation led them to underplay the doctrine of the Atonement understood as God's provision in Christ of a sacrificial offering whereby we are rescued from sin and death. Candlish and Bomberger felt that their respective contestants did minimise the dire consequences of sin and the requirements of holy, gracious law; and, for all the benefits which flow from the restoration by Maurice and Nevin of *grace* as the first word of the gospel, not sin, I have to agree that Candlish and Bomberger have a point in their favour. Their emphasis upon the transcendent holiness and righteousness of God, and upon our sin and need of rescue, and their consequent protest against any understanding of Incarnation which seems to set us automatically in a process of redemption and, at worst, can seem to bypass the historic Cross, cannot lightly be set aside.

As for the twentieth-century mythographers, we saw that they were motivated in part by the increasingly important claims and challenges of a world perceived as religiously pluralistic. They sought to restate a view of the Incarnation as a truth-bearing myth, and did so with relatively little — and then inadequate — reference to the Atonement. While they proclaimed a God who identifies himself with human suffering, they did not relate this notion strongly to holiness, sin and saving grace. As a result, their understanding of Christ was impoverished.

If undue emphasis is placed upon Incarnation conceived as process, or as the enacting of the eternal principle that God is with us in all the vicissitudes of life, we can overlook what Forsyth bluntly expressed thus: "Man's need determined God's deed."[80] Again, if we over-emphasize the idea that in Christ the victory is already won (as Christians believe it is), we can even come to believe that sin and evil are inevitable stages on the way to good, whereas, as James Orr thundered, "Sin is that which ought not to be *at all*."[81] Undue emphasis upon our union with Christ in the Incarnation can lead to a doctrine of the Church as the continuation of the Incarnation which forgets that the churches we know are always earthen vessels composed of sinners. Again, if the Incarnation comes to be understood as a symbol witnessing to God's immanence within humanity, what becomes of the message of salvation which is the heartbeat of Christian mission?[82]

But what is most at risk in all such over-emphases is, as we have seen, the doctrine of the person of Christ. For if we have no clear idea of what God-in-Christ has done in the Cross-Resurrection event, we shall in the end have a reduced view of who Christ is. This is the point I wish to reaffirm in conclusion. Let me do this by placing side by side the Anglican Clement Webb and the Congregationalist P.T. Forsyth. Webb prefers the doctrinal emphasis to fall upon the Incarnation, not upon the Atonement. He writes: "It has often been observed that, of the great Christian dogmas, Evangelicalism laid stress especially on the Atonement, Tractarianism on the Incarnation. It is easy to see that it is the latter emphasis rather than the former that tends to the encouragement of all the higher human activities as capable of sanctification through the taking of our manhood into God."[83] Over against this Forsyth declares, "Any theology that places us in a spiritual *process*, or native movement between the finite and the infinite, depreciates the value of spiritual *act*, and thus makes us independent of the grace of God. Its movement is processional, spectacular, aesthetic, it is not historic, dramatic, tragic or ethical."[84]

It will be clear that on this point I side with Forsyth, though I do think that the Reformed tradition, for example — and for all kinds of contextual reasons — has traditionally taken a needlessly dismal view of what Webb calls "the higher human activities," and to this extent I am with him. But if I am on balance with Forsyth, I am in good ecumenical company too. The Scottish Presbyterian James Denney insisted that "the rationale of the incarnation is in the atonement."[85] A contemporary Roman Catholic theologian, Thomas Marsh, has well said that the "origin of Christology in the soteriological question and experience must be respected in systematic theology and its determining influence allowed just scope."[86] And although there is an Anglican line from Maurice to Webb and beyond which is unduly weighted towards the Incarnation at the expense of the Atonement, many other Anglicans have seen the warning lights. To take just one example: in an interesting article J.A. Baker claims that "part at least of the essence of Christianity as such...must be whatever central tenet it does not share with any other faith; and that is one thing only, the classical doctrine of the Incarnation."[87] So far he sounds like Maurice and Mercersburg. But, when Canon Baker wishes to counter those Christians who prefer a God who is like Jesus with the classical doctrine of the Incarnation, he comes to our very point: "The thing which gave Christianity its wide-ranging appeal was that it offered not a revelation of what God was like, but a salvation through what God had done."[88] He clinches his argument thus: "If indeed 'God was in Christ reconciling the world to himself,' then God must be so intimately involved with Jesus that what was done had really been done by God in person."[89]

Another Anglican, Stephen Sykes, is right to draw our attention to the fact that in the New Testament itself there are different ways of speaking of God's action in Christ. He refers to the priest-victim stories in the Biblical text. In the priest stories Christ offers himself to God; in the victim stories, God lovingly provides a sacrifice for sin.[90] Nevertheless Robert Watts was not wide of the mark in insisting that in the letter to the Hebrews, "our Saviour's assumption of the nature of the sons of God...is represented as subordinate to the expiation of their sins," while for his part Paul "does not single out the incarnation as the ground of his glorying. On the contrary, he emphasises the cross and the crucifixion, and avows his determination to know nothing among those to whom he ministered save Jesus Christ and Him crucified."[91]

Almost one hundred years ago the eminent theologian and preacher, R.W. Dale, threw down the gauntlet thus: "Who can this be through whom the sins of the race are forgiven, through whose death we ourselves have received the forgiveness of sins...Who is he?...If you shrink from calling Him God, what other title adequate to the greatness of His work will you attribute to Him?"[92] Sixteen hundred years earlier Athanasius stood against the world and asked similar questions: "*Who* was it that was needed for such grace and such recall as we required? Who, save the Word of God Himself...?...For He alone, being Word of the Father and above all, was in consequence both able to recreate all, and worthy to suffer on behalf of all and to be an ambassador for all with the Father."[93]

If we would maintain even the relative doctrinal integrity of which we are capable, we should do well to stand with Athanasius. What has Christ done? Then who must he be? The answer lies in the realization that God alone can save.

NOTES

1. Thomas Watson, *A Body of Divinity*, rev.ed. (London: The Banner of Truth Trust, 1965), 1.

2. Ibid., 5.

3. Thomas Aquinas, *The Summa Theologica*, I, Q I, art. i.

4. Ibid., Q I, art. ii.

5. Samuel Hopkins, *The System of Doctrines Contained in Divine Revelation Explained and Defended*, 2nd. ed. (Boston: Lincoln and Edmonds, 1811), 3.

6. John Gill, *Complete Body of Doctrinal and Practical Divinity* (1767–70; Grand Rapids: Baker Book House, 1978), I: viii.

7. David Bogue and James Bennett, *History of Dissenters,* 1808, IV:467.

8. G.H. Clark, *What Do Presbyterians Believe?* (Philadelphia: Presbyterian & Reformed, 1965), 47, 172.

9. Nathanael Emmons, *Works* (Boston: Crocker & Brewster, 1842), I: 193.

10. Robert Watts, "Progress in theology," *The Catholic Presbyterian* IX (April 1883): 295.

11. See e.g. Holmes Rolston III, *John Calvin Versus the Westminster Confession* (Richmond: John Knox Press, 1972); R.T. Kendall, *Calvin and English Calvinism to 1649*, (London: Oxford University Press, 1979); Paul Helm, *Calvin and the Calvinists*, (Edinburgh: The Banner of Truth Trust, 1982); J.B. Torrance, "Covenant or Contract? A Study of the Theological Background of Worship in Seventeenth-Century Scotland," *Scottish Journal of Theology* XXIII (1970): 51–76; idem, "The Contribution of McLeod Campbell to Scottish Theology," ibid., XXVI (1973: 295–311; idem, "Calvinism and Puritanism in England and Scotland: Some Basic Concepts in the Development of Federal Theology," in *Calvinus Reformator*, Potchefstroom University for Christian Higher Education, 1982, 264–86; idem, "Strengths and weaknesses of the Westminster theology," in *The Westminster Confession in the Church Today*, ed. A.I.C. Heron (Edinburgh: The Saint Andrew Press, 1982), 40–54.

12. William Jay, *Autobiography*, ed. George Redford and John Angell James (1854; reprint, Edinburgh: The Banner of Truth Trust, 1974), 170.

13. Ibid., 472.

14. Isaiah 55: 8–9.

15. Vernon F. Storr, *The Development of English Theology in the Nineteenth Century*, (London: Longmans, 1913), 217.

16. P.T. Forsyth, *The Person and Place of Jesus Christ* (1909; reprint, London: Independent Press 1961), 15.

17. James Orr, *The Progress of Dogma* (London: James Clarke [1901]), 8–9.

18. J. Gill, op.cit., xiv.

19. J. Orr, op.cit., 24–32.

20. P.T. Forsyth, *The Church and the Sacraments* (1917; reprint, London: Independent Press, 1947), 83.

21. H.R. Mackintosh, *Some Aspects of Christian Belief* (London: Hodder & Stoughton [1923]), 176.

22. *Hymns...by the Rev. Joseph Hart* (Cranbrook: J.T. Dennett, 1871 ed.), no. 55.

23. J. McLeod Campbell, *The Nature of the Atonement* (London: Macmillan, 2nd ed. 1867), xiii.

24. For which see further Alan P.F. Sell, *Theology in Turmoil. The Roots, Course and Significance of the Conservative-Liberal Debate in Modern Theology* (Grand Rapids: Baker Book House, 1986).

25. Benjamin Jowett, "On Atonement and Satisfaction," quoted by B.M.G. Reardon, *Religious Thought in the Victorian Age* (London: Longmans, 1971), 334.

26. J. McLeod Campbell had come to precisely the same realization in Scotland.

27. A powerful protest against this was entered by the Methodist theologian, J. Scott Lidgett (1854–1953). See e.g. his *The Spiritual Principle of the Atonement*, 1897; *The Fatherhood of God*, 1903; *The Victorian Transformation of Theology*, 1934. It must be admitted, however, the some liberal theologians so sentimentalized the idea of the Fatherhood of God as to raise the question, "If God is *so* pleasant and benign, why the Cross at all?" In a word, the *holiness* of his love was played down, or neglected altogether.

28. See *The Nature of the Atonement*; and George M. Tuttle, *So Rich a Soil. John McLeod Campbell on Christian Atonement* (Edinburgh: The Handsel Press, 1986).

29. Calvin, *Institute*, II, xvi, 5.

30. Quoted by John Ferguson in *Reform* (February, 1975): 11.

31. B.F. Westcott, *The Gospel of Life* (London: Macmillan, 1892), xxi.

32. This controversy was somewhat one-sided. Candlish regretted that Maurice made no reply to his detailed criticisms.

33. F.D. Maurice, *The Lord's Prayer. Nine Sermons Preached in the Chapel of Lincoln's Inn* (London: J.W. Parker, 1848), 48.

34. F.D. Maurice, *Theological Essays* (Cambridge: Macmillan, 1853), 147.

35. *The Life of F.D. Maurice, Chiefly Told in his Own Letters*, ed. Frederick Maurice [son] (London: Macmillan, 1884), II: 631.

36. See e.g., D.W. Simon's assessment in his *The Redemption of Man*, (Edinburgh: T. & T. Clark, 1889), 35–6.

37. Robert Mackintosh, *Historic Theories of Atonement* (London, Hodder & Stoughton, 1920), 203. Cf. P.T. Forsyth, *The Work of Christ* (1910; reprint,

London: Independent Press, 1958), 99: "The real objective element in the atonement is not that something was offered to God, but that God made the offering."

38. R.S. Candlish, *An Examination of Mr. Maurice's Theological Essays* (London: James Nisbet, 1854), 2.

39. Ibid., 11.

40. Ibid., 14.

41. Ibid., 17.

42. Ibid., 35.

43. Ibid., 225.

44. Ibid., 229, 230–31.

45. R.S. Candlish, *Mr. Maurice's Theology. A Letter to the Right Hon. The Earl of Shaftesbury* (London: James Nisbet, 1860), 15.

46. B.M.G. Reardon, *Religious Thought in the Victorian Age*, 194. Both Dr. Reardon (168–70) and V.F. Storr, *The Development of English Theology* (344–7), find the strictures of the Methodist J.H. Rigg (*Modern Anglican Theology*, 1859) wide of the mark; so do we. Rigg claimed undue Platonic influence upon Maurice's theology. While a Platonist thrust cannot be denied, Maurice contended *for* a historically-grounded revelation, and *against* the "theology of consciousness." See his *Theological Essays*, Ch. VII. Hugh Martin adjudicated the Candlish-Maurice debate in Candlish's favour thus: "it is unnecessary to say that [Candlish] has received, and will receive, no answer to his minute and masterly polemic." See H. Martin, *The Atonement* (1870; reprint, Edinburgh: John Knox Press, 1976), 255. For a study of Candlish guarding his other flank see Edward McKinley, *The Relation of Incarnation to Atonement in the Christology of R.S. Candlish, and its Contribution to the Development of Scottish Theology*, unpublished doctoral dissertation, University of Edinburgh, 1966. Candlish is here shown to be an opponent of the federal theologians' theory of the passive obedience of Christ, and an exponent of the view that the Atonement was wrought by the whole course of Christ's obedience.

47. For the movement at large see James H. Nichols, ed., *The Mercersburg Theology* (New York: Oxford University Press, 1966). See also *The New Mercersburg Review*, from 1985 onwards.

48. For Schaff, see George H. Shriver, *Philip Schaff, Christian Scholar and Ecumenical Prophet* (Macon GA: Mercer University Press, 1987).

49. See e.g. "Another Victim of Nevinism [i.e. the Rev. E.O. Forney]," *The Reformed Church Monthly* VI (1873): 413ff. The *Monthly*, which ran from 1886–77 was founded in opposition to the Mercersburg Theology, and edited by J.H.A. Bomberger.

50. See Calvin D. Yost, *Ursinus College. A History of its First Hundred Years* (Collegeville, PA: Ursinus College, 1985).

51. See J.H.A. Bomberger, "Dr. Nevin and his Antagonists," *The Mercersburg Review* V (1853): 89–124; 145–181.

52. J.W. Nevin, "Wilberforce on the Incarnation," *The Mercersburg Review* II (1850); quoted by J.H. Nichols, op.cit., 79.

53. J.W. Nevin, *Answer to Professor Dorner*, (Philadelphia: S.R. Fisher, 1868), 23.

54. Ibid., 69.

55. Ibid., 70–71.

56. J.W. Nevin, *The Mystical Presence*, ed. Bard Thompson and George H. Bricker (1846; reprint, Philadelphia: United Church Press, 1966), 163.

57. I.A. Dorner, *The Liturgical Conflict in the Reformed Church of North America* (Philadelphia: Loag, 1868), 17.

58. J.H.A. Bomberger, "The Great Contrast," *The Reformed Church Monthly* IV (1871): 368. See further, James I. Good, "Theological Views," in *The Rev. J.H.A. Bomberger, Doctor of Divinity, Doctor of Laws, 1817–1890* (Philadelphia: Publications and Sunday School Board of the Reformed Church in the U.S., 1917), 251–267.

59. F.F. Bahner, *Bomberger Memorial Discourse*, delivered in Trinity Reformed Church, Waynesboro, PA, Sunday 14 September 1890, 3. I should like to thank Mrs. Florence M. Bricker, of the Evangelical and Reformed Library and Archives, Lancaster Theological Seminary, PA, for her assistance in locating Bomberger documents and pamphlets; also the Canadian Social Sciences and Humanities Research Council for funding a journey to Lancaster, PA.

60. Quoted in T.H. Darlow, *William Robertson Nicoll. Life and Letters* (London: Hodder & Stoughton, 1925), 160.

61. *The Myth of God Incarnate*, ed. John Hick (London: SCM Press, 1977), ix.

62. Maurice Wiles, ibid., 5.

63. Ibid., ix.

64. Cf. the comment by Basil Mitchell in *Incarnation and Myth*, ed. Michael Goulder (London: SCM Press, 1979), 240: "I feel bound to ask whether enough account has been taken in the mythographers' approach of what is implied by divine transcendence."

65. J. Hick, *The Myth*, 176.

66. Frances Young, ibid., 18–19.

67. Ibid., 30.

68. Ibid.

69. Ibid, 34–5.

70. Romans 5: 8; II Corinthians 5: 19.

71. J. Hick, *Incarnation and Myth*, 82.

72. *The Myth*, x.

73. F. Young, ibid., 47.

74. James Martineau, *Essays, Reviews and Addresses* (London: Longman, Green, 1891), II: 443.

75. Arthur J. Long, "Recent Theological Discussion," *Faith and Freedom* XXXIV (Autumn 1980): 16. John Macquarrie was stern on the point: "It would be an anachronism to describe the positions in this book as Arian, deist or Unitarian, but unquestionably there are affinities, and it is hardly likely that an updated Christianity without incarnation will prove any more successful than these dead ends of the past." In *The Truth of God Incarnate*, ed. Michael Green (London: Hodder & Stoughton, 1977), 144.

76. M. Wiles, *The Myth*, 8–9.

77. Cf. Alan P.F. Sell, "Autonomy, Immanence and the Loss of Authority," *Churchman* XCVI (1982): 123–141, for some comments on the somewhat earlier

views of Dr. Wiles. With slight modifications, I would stand by what I then wrote. I should, however, like to make clear my indebtedness to Dr. Wiles for the stimulus and challenge I have derived from his writings. Others who pursued the mythographers at the time include Michael Green and the authors of *The Truth of God Incarnate*; A.I.C. Heron in *Scottish Journal of Theology* XXXI (1978): 51–71; H.P. Owen in *Religious Studies* XIII (1977): 491–7. The debate found its way into the popular religious press and, e.g. with respect to John Hick the question of church discipline was raised by Norman Birnie and C.E.B. Cranfield. See *Reform*, "Letters," September and December 1977 respectively. See also Robert Crawford, *The Saga of God Incarnate* rev.ed. (Edinburgh: T. & T. Clark, 1987).

78. B. Jowett, *Essay and Dissertations*, quoted by B.M.G. Reardon, *Religious Thought in the Victorian Age*, 334.

79. P.T. Forsyth, *The Work of Christ* (1910; reprint, London: Independent Press, 1958), 228–9.

80. P.T. Forsyth, *The Person and Place of Jesus Christ*, 220.

81. James Orr, *Sidelights on Christian Doctrine* (London: Marshall,1909), 94; cf. *The Christian View of God and the World*, 4th ed. (Edinburgh: Eliot, 1897), 171.

82. This concern was long ago expressed by A.E. Garvie (no conservative reactionary) in *The Missionary Obligation in the Light of the Changes of Modern Thought* (London: Hodder & Stoughton, 1914), 65–9.

83. C.C.J. Webb, *A Century of Anglican Theology and Other Lectures* (Oxford: Blackwell, 1923), 39.

84. P.T. Forsyth, *Positive Preaching and the Modern Mind* (1907; reprint, London: Independent Press, 1964), 146.

85. J. Denney, *The Christian Doctrine of Reconciliation* (London: Hodder & Stoughton, 1917), 65.

86. Thomas Marsh, "Soteriology Today," *The Irish Theological Quarterly* XLVI, 3, (1979): 147.

87. J.A. Baker, "The Essence of Christianity," *The Expository Times* LXXXVII (1975): 36.

88. Ibid., 37.

89. Ibid., 37. It is by no means suggested that Anglicans alone emphasized the Incarnation at the expense of the Atonement. On the contrary, the distinguished Congregationalist, R.W. Dale — influenced by F.D. Maurice — did precisely that *when contrasting his own evangelicalism with that of earlier years*: "The incarnation, with all that it reveals concerning God, man, and the universe, concerning this life and the life to come, stands first; with the early Evangelicals the Death of Christ for human sin stood first...In theology the Incarnation lies deeper than the Atonement; and the great and august mystery of the Trinity lies deeper than the Incarnation." See his *The Old Evangelicalism and the New* (London: Hodder & Stoughton, 1889), 48–9. However, Dale had also written quite conservatively on *The Atonement* (1875), editions of which work were appearing for some time after the publication of *The Old Evangelicalism*... My own view is that (*contra some* older evangelicals) the *grace* of God, most fully active in the Cross-Resurrection event, comes first; and that (*contra* Dale — at times), we see our need most clearly in the light of that event. Of course, as I have also stated, the Atonement presupposes the Incarnation and is not to be sundered from it; and both are the action of the Triune God.

90. S.W. Sykes, "The Strange Persistence of Kenotic Christology," in *Being and Truth. Essays in Honour of John Macquarrie* (London: SCM Press, 1986), 368.

91. Robert Watts, "Progress in Theology," op. cit., 291.

92. R.W. Dale, *Christian Doctrine* (1894; reprint, London: Hodder & Stoughton, 1903), 114.

93. *St. Athanasius on the Incarnation*, trans. and ed. by A Religious of CSMV, 2nd ed. (London: Mowbray, 1963), 33.

ETHICAL INTEGRITY

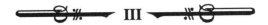

III

ETHICAL INTEGRITY

The J. Louis Lebel Lecture

Henry Grove (1683–1738) was tutor at the Dissenting Academy in Taunton, Somerset. He was regarded with suspicion by some of his high Calvinist peers, for he believed in allowing his students to think for themselves; he upheld the place of reason in religion in the face of those whom he regarded as doctrinaire bigots. The fact that a number of his students thought their way into the so-called Arianism of the eighteenth century did little to commend Grove to such opponents as the venerable John Ball of Honiton.[1]

Grove's favourite subject was ethics. He declared that "all Morality has its foundation in Religion, or the belief of a Supreme Being."[2] This was the traditional view and, consistently with it, ethics had been regarded as an integral part of theology. Hence the various Bodies of Practical Divinity which, after the manner of the Ten Commandments and the summary of them, "Love God, love neighbour," drew ethics out of doctrine.

Despite the fact that, intellectually, Grove held doctrine and ethics together, he introduced a curriculum development at Taunton: he divorced the theology class from the ethics class and thus innocently took a step which was to lead to the divorce of ethics from religion with which we today are so familiar. The importance of Henry Grove is that he was one of the first, if not the first, to divide the subject-matter in this way.

One way of attempting to take stock of the present situation is to ask the question, Is there such a thing as Christian ethics? If the question means, Is there a subject of study named Christian ethics? the answer is clearly in the affirmative, for there exist teachers and students of the subject so named. We may still ask, of course, whether such a subject has a right to exist, or whether it is not in some respects a pseudo-subject. Again, if by "Christian ethics" we mean the ethical behaviour and/or reflection of Christians, then clearly we can point to examples of the ethical behaviour and thought of Christians. But if we were to suppose that Christian ethics labels a territory of moral reflection and endeavour which is absolutely removed from all other ethical territories, then, I think, we should be making a serious mistake. For there is not in that sense a Christian ethic distinct from all other ethics — any more than there is a Christian mathematics distinct from all other mathematics. Furthermore, just as a person who is not a Christian may score 100 percent in mathematics, while a Christian may score zero percent, so a non-Christian may make admirable moral choices while a Christian continually demonstrates the not-very-noble art of backsliding!

Without condoning habitual backsliders, they do at least remind us that at its heart Christianity is a word of salvation for sinners, and not simply a series of ethical tests of which paragons of virtue may attempt four in three hours. Paul was being no more than realistic when he confessed that the problem is often not that we do not know what we should do, but that we do not do it: "The good which I want to do," he wrote to the Romans, "I fail to do; but what I do is the wrong which is against my will" — and this because of the continuing influence of sin in his life.[3] To people in this position the exhortations of a moral teacher appear only as an additional burden which utterly misses the point. "Miserable creature that I am," Paul continues, "who is there to rescue me...?" Rescue, not further advice, is required. And who is the rescuer? "God alone," he cries, "through Jesus Christ our Lord. Thanks be to God!"[4]

Here we approach the heart of the matter. Although ethics is an autonomous field — and were it not so, we could not without circularity resort to it for pointers to the existence of God;[5] were it not so, we could not find common ethical ground with humanists, or with people of other faiths (as I shall shortly contend that we can) — Christians can and should view moral matters in the light of their Christian view of the world. And at the heart of that view of the world is a God who in Christ saves to the uttermost and, by his Holy Spirit, empowers the new life which he creates. As Sydney Cave wrote forty years ago, "Christianity is both gift and demand. But even to begin to meet the demand we must first receive the gift."[6]

The Christian's ethical reflection and praxis is prompted by gratitude to God. I call two witnesses. The first is the seventeenth-century Richard Baxter: "Let Thankfulness to God thy Creator, Redeemer and Regenerator, be the very temperament of thy soul, and faithfully expressed by thy tongue and life."[7] The second witness is the present-day English Methodist scholar John Munsey Turner, who exhorts us to return to the idea that we stand right before God not because of what we do, but because of his grace — his overflowing love towards the undeserving. Such a return, he suggests, "might save us from the awful guilt-ridden 'frantic philanthropy' which seems to be a substitute for gospel these days. Our concern for others should stem not from our guilt about the supposed sins of our imperialist grandparents but from 'the wonder why such love for me.' Anything less can lead to pharisaic self-righteousness."[8]

In a word, Christian ethical reflection will be theological reflection; and Christian praxis will be devotional praxis — it will flow from gratitude to God. In Christian ethical theory, gift and demand will be held together as an indissoluble whole; in Christian praxis there will be a constant concern — a striving — to ensure that the actions performed are consistent with the gospel proclaimed. Some of Jesus's sternest words were reserved for those who professed one thing and did another. He called them by their proper name: hypocrites, play-actors.[9]

In attempting to sketch in more detail what it means for there to be integrity concerning gospel, ethical reflection and practice I must be highly selective. G.F. Woods rightly said that "any defence of theological ethics must be made on the basis of the whole system of Christian doctrine."[10] It takes only a moment's thought to realize that there is no Christian doctrine which does not have ethical implications. The doctrine of creation leads us into questions of the stewardship of the created order, and into those pressing ecological issues about which we hear so much and sometimes seem to do so little. Christian doctrines concerning the last things and the ongoing judgment import an urgency into our ethical thinking and behaviour, and require us to view matters under the aspect of eternity. Or again, one scholar has recently offered a Christian perspective on ethics which sets out from the concepts of freedom and obedience, while another has developed his ethical thinking on the key concept of Christ's resurrection from the dead.[11] I shall attempt to illustrate my contention that Christian ethical reflection is theological reflection, and that Christian praxis of integrity is praxis under the gospel by reference to the concept of love (*agape*) and in relation to a specific issue, apartheid.[12]

I

Dr. Kingsley Barrett, among others, has pointed out with reference to the terms *agapan* and *agape* that "there is little in profane Greek, or in the LXX, to illuminate their meaning in the New Testament."[13] New Testament scholars are thus led to seek for the distinctive features of *agape*, and to contrast *agape* with such other Greek words for loving and liking as *philia, storge, philadelphia, philanthropia* and, above all, *eros*. As compared with *agape, eros* has sometimes received a bad press, especially, some would declare, at the hands of Anders Nygren in his *Agape and Eros* (1932–8), for he claimed an absolute disjunction between *agape* and *eros*. What seems clear is that although in Classical Greek *eros* is used to refer primarily to sexual love, it is also, not least in Plato and Aristotle, used of the longing of the soul for union with the divine. But, whether used literally or metaphorically, *eros* is always prompted by the worth of its object. Here we find the locus of the most profound and legitimate distinction between *eros* and *agape*, and none has put the point more plainly than Paul: "Christ died for us while we were yet *sinners*, and that is God's own proof of his love towards us."[14]

It is in the Johannine writings above all that we find emphasis upon God's essential nature as *agape*. God is love is a recurring theme in I John, for example. We cannot stop there, however, for although there are the makings of a gospel in those words, there is no good news until John 3:16 is fulfilled; on which verse William Temple commented: "This is the heart of the Gospel. Not 'God is love' — a precious truth, but affirming no divine act for our redemption. *God so loved that he gave...He gave*; it was an act, not only a continuing mood of generosity."[15] The love of God, which is redemptive and victorious, is paradigmatically manifested and supremely active in the Cross-Resurrection event. It was as a result of that event that Paul could rejoice that "nothing...can separate us from the love of God in Christ Jesus our Lord."[16]

God's *agape*, then, is no abstract love; it is a love which finds its clearest expression on the stage of human history, and in the course of meeting the worst in that history. Small wonder that Paul cannot speak of *agape* except in relation to the Cross. There was wrought the unrepeatable act of love.[17] At the Cross love was not merely demonstrated, it was at work. How different is all this from the view that Jesus Christ is just a great — even the supreme — moral teacher. As Robert Mackintosh sardonically wrote, "A Christ who has no functions except Addisonian essays and gentle moral suasion, is not a Christ."[18] We might say that *agape* needs to be seen in order to be believed; but it needs to act in order to be redemptive.

This redemptive *agape*, which calls forth love and gratitude and makes possible our loving response, is the ground of new life. From the human side, as the Puritan Thomas Watson put it picturesquely, "Love is to the soul as the weights to the clock, it sets the soul a-going towards God, as the wings by which we fly to heaven. By love we cleave to God, as the needle to the loadstone."[19] But this human response is not (as Watson's words taken out of context might imply) simply an aspiration of the soul. It is obediential. This love is commanded of us by Jesus: "I give you a new commandment; love one another; as I have loved you, so you are to love one another."[20] As C.H. Dodd pointed out, this love is no sentimental feeling, for feelings cannot be commanded; it is "primarily an active determination of the will."[21] If, as T.W. Manson remarked, the Great commandment — love God, love neighbour — is the quintessence of Jewish ethics, the words "as I have loved you" indicate the heart of Christian ethics.[22] And although in John's gospel the new commandment is uttered in relation to the bearing of disciples towards one another, this is only because the writer sees them as God's vanguard. He has by no means forgotten that God so loved the world. Rather, the world is to be reached by the calibre of love which Christians show to each other and demonstrate to the world. On which theme William Temple wryly commented, "When the Church keeps the New Commandment, the world may keep the Old."[23]

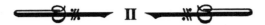

II

I hope that what I have said so far illustrates the truth of E.P. Dickie's remark that "the divine initiative precedes the divine imperative."[24] Precedes it, yes; but the two are inseparable. Let me now, therefore, attempt to show how, in relation to a specific issue, Christian ethical reflection and action is informed by the gospel, in particular, by *agape*. The issue in question is that of apartheid in South Africa.

I hardly need to remind you that the policy of apartheid, or separate development, is, according to its proponents, designed to enable those of differing racial groups to develop their full potential in their own way, at their own pace, and in their own place. A biblical and theological justification of this policy has been provided over the years by some Reformed theologians and others, and the policy itself has been pursued in ways which can only be described as brutal and dehumanizing. The ten so-called homelands were reserved for ten separate communities, and the relocations policy has brought untold suffering in its wake. Mixed marriages were forbidden, racial separation in public place was enforced unilaterally, families were broken up, and many lost hope. In the last few years some modifications of the policy have been introduced which, in turn, have engendered an ultra-conservative backlash.

A number of Christian bodies have protested against apartheid, and I wish to refer to the "Resolution on Racism and South Africa" of the World Alliance of Reformed Churches. This resolution was adopted at the Alliance's General Council meeting at Ottawa, 1982. My reason for selecting this resolution is that the Reformed family, a major Christian communion of some seventy million Christians, has felt particularly uneasy about the fact that so many of the theological justifications of apartheid have been produced by white Dutch Reformed theologians in South Africa. The Alliance, of course, opposes racism wherever it is to be found; but here was racism being justified theologically by some of its own people. In no sudden way, but only after more than twenty years of conversations, the Alliance's General Council passed its resolution, from which I now quote:

God in Jesus Christ has affirmed human dignity. Through his life, death and resurrection he has reconciled people to God and to themselves. He has broken down the wall of partition and enmity and has become our peace. He is the Lord of His church who has brought us together in one Lord, one faith, one baptism, one God who is the father of us all (Eph. 4: 5, 6).

The Gospel of Jesus Christ demands, therefore, a community of believers which transcends all barriers of race — a community in which the love of Christ and for one another has overcome the divisions of race and colour.

The Gospel confronts racism, which is in its very essence a form of idolatry. Racism fosters a false sense of supremacy, it denies the common humanity of believers, and it denies Christ's reconciling, humanising work. It systematises oppression, domination and injustice. As such the struggle against racism, wherever it is found, in overt and covert forms, is a responsibility laid upon the church by the Gospel of Jesus Christ in every country and society.

At the present time, without denying the universality of racist sin, we must call special attention to South Africa. Apartheid (or "Separate Development") in South Africa poses a unique challenge to the Church, especially the churches of the Reformed tradition. The white Afrikaans Reformed Churches of South Africa through the years have worked out in considerable detail both the policy itself and the theological and moral justification for the system. Apartheid...is therefore a pseudo-religious ideology as well as a political policy. It depends to a large extent on this moral and theological justification. The division of Reformed Churches of South Africa on the basis of race and colour is being defended as a faithful interpretation of the will of God and of the Reformed understanding of the church in the world. This leads to the division of Christians at the table of the Lord as a matter of practice and policy, which has been continually affirmed save for exceptional circumstances under special permission by the white Afrikaans Reformed Churches...

...we regard [apartheid] as an issue on which it is not possible to differ without seriously jeopardizing the integrity of our common confession as Reformed Churches.

We declare, with Black Reformed Christians of South Africa that apartheid ("Separate Development") is a sin, and that the moral and theological justification of it is a travesty of the Gospel, and in its persistent disobedience to the word of God, a theological heresy...[25]

On the basis of this theological and biblical reflection the Resolution proceeds to call for the suspension of two white Afrikaans churches from the World Alliance of Reformed Churches until such time as they have taken steps to repudiate apartheid and to mitigate its baneful effects; and it challenges all the member churches around the world to deal with the racism in their midst. Shortly afterwards the Lutheran World Federation took similar action in respect of some of its South African member churches.

Now it is only proper to point out that within the suspended churches some have been working for change, and that changes have indeed taken place in certain areas. I do not wish to pursue the question of apartheid for its own sake. I have introduced this Resolution because it provides a crystal clear example of the way in which a body of Christians, after serious and solemn reflection upon God's *agape*, which frees and unites and breaks down the walls of separation between all sorts and conditions of people, was led to make a moral judgment, to articulate an ethical protest in the name of the Gospel, and to take actions consistent with that protest. Doctrine and ethics, profession and praxis, were seen to be an integrated whole; the reception of the gift of grace was seen to entail an obedient response in a specific moral context. (The Resolution will still exemplify these points when actual apartheid policies are no longer in force.) Heresy is a distortion of Christian truth, and the solemn declaration was made that if apartheid is a sin — something utterly alien to God — then the attempted theological defence of that sin cannot but land one in heresy. For in seeking to defend apartheid theologically you cannot but deny the Christian doctrines of humanity (for we are one in Christ), the Church (for we are one at the Table of the Lord), creation (for we are all alike in God's image), redemption (for we are all saved by the one blood), and eschatology (for heaven knows no racist barriers).

Not the least important aspect of the Resolution is the fact that it allows no room to that patronizing arrogance which would prompt us to thank God that we are not like other men, or even as those Afrikaaners. You may have heard of the Sunday School teacher who was relating the story of the Pharisee and the Publican to his class. You will recall that the Pharisee thanked God that he was not like other men; the publican would not so much as lift his eyes to heaven, but pray for mercy. At the end of the story the teacher said, "Now, children, we shall say a prayer; and in our prayer we shall thank God that we are not like the Pharisee!" It's quite amusing — until you realise that you are probably thinking, "Thank God I'm not like the Sunday School teacher!" You see how easy it is to see the sins of others while being blind to our own. The "Resolution on Racism and South Africa" challenges Reformed Christians around the world to deal with the racism in their midst.

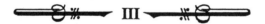 III

From the many issues which the Resolution raises I shall now select three for comment. The first concerns the idea of collective moral responsibility. There can be no doubt that many churchly ethical pronouncements presuppose a doctrine of collective responsibility, and it is not difficult to see why. The Biblical doctrine of creation posits the solidarity of humanity created in the image of God. The Biblical idea of a covenant between God and people — a covenant created on the initiative of God — and of a renewed covenant sealed by the blood of Christ, suggests the obligations of fellowship. The "Resolution on Racism and South Africa" quotes Calvin on this matter, and he, in turn, is echoing I John: "None of the brethren can be injured, despised, rejected, abused, or any way offended by us, without at the same time injuring, despising and abusing Christ by the wrongs we do...We cannot love Christ without loving Him in the brethren."[26] For this reason we cannot tolerate the privatization of ethics. We have to agree with John Donne that "No man is an Island, entire of itself,"[27]

and to deny the ethical justification of so many in these days: "So long as you're not hurting anyone else..."

But from none of these insights need we infer that I am objectively morally responsible for what someone else is doing or has done (perhaps long ago). The truth of this observation is thrown into relief if we consider what suffices to exonerate a person. Someone may have the theoretical capacity to do good; but if he is not aware of the need and is not wilfully ignorant of it, or if he is restrained by force of some kind so that he cannot assist, then he is not culpable. As Aristotle said long ago, praise and blame attach to voluntary actions; and voluntary actions are those which are not compelled, and which are done with knowledge of the circumstances.[28] But if someone has the capacity to do good; knowledge that an appropriate action is called for; and is in no way restrained — either by force, or by the clash of temporally coincident *prima facie* duties — then, if the person *chooses* not to do good he is culpable. In such a case it would not be a defence to say that failure to act was caused by one's membership of a sinful race; or because we are caught up in sinful structures (which, after all, cannot repent — though sinful *people*, who hold such structures in place, can and do repent, sometimes corporately); or because our failure to act was somehow determined by our character, or is attributable to parental neglect when we are young, and the like. For to explain how one has come to be as one is, is not to shelve responsibility for failure to act (or, conversely, for acting). To suppose otherwise is to dehumanize the person by suggesting that he is so prone to influences, or so programmed by his past, as to be incapable of being a *moral* agent: he becomes a robot.

In passing we may note that if a person is sufficiently competent to diagnose the factors which have gone into making him what he is, and if he does not like what he sees, then he is more than ever culpable if he does not take steps to mend his ways. This is not to deny that some environments may in principle — though not always in practice, as witness lordly rogues — be conducive to high moral standards, while others, such as those which, to cite J.H. Muirhead's now quaint-sounding list, include "brothels, gambling dens, cribs and finishing schools"[29] appear to militate against them. It is simply to assert that we are not so inhuman as to be incapable of decision and choice (granted the possession of our faculties), and therefore of being liable to praise and blame.

But in insisting upon the moral responsibility of the individual, am I not denying the import of those religious notions of solidarity to which I earlier alluded? Not at all. If I am not responsible for the actual deeds perpetrated by a tyrannical regime on another continent, I am responsible for my actions, or lack of actions, respecting the pressurizing of my elected representative, the refusal to buy the offender's exported goods, and so on. Even here, however, we must be realistic, for on the one hand we have too much information, on the other hand too little. Thus, on the one hand, the worthy cannot but be daunted by the sheer amount of information which nowadays bombards them. It would be a more than full-time task to pursue with the relevant authorities all of the pressing issues presented in one issue of a serious Sunday newspaper (a problem which, presumably, does not confront sabbatarians of integrity). On the other hand, the amount of research which a diligent pacifist might need to undertake in order to discover who owns whom, so that monies would not be invested in companies which are involved in the production of weapons might be of doctoral thesis proportions. And all of this wading through of information, or seeking out of information, has to be done in a situation in which duties conflict. We must do what we can about tyranny and peace; but we must also earn bread to feed our family; attend worship; correspond with absent friends; or, tend the Oxfam stall. And all the time we must be aware of the temptation of finding it easier to write to our M.P. about the evils rampant on some distant shore than to attend to the beggar at our gate; and of succumbing to that disenchantment with politics which leads to apathy and allows wicked powers to make hay.

One slightly different aspect of the problem needs to be noted, and the point has been well expressed by Henry Stob:

> When an individual joins a voluntary organization he is, as long as he remains a member of that organization, co-responsible for the actions taken by that organization. If the actions are evil, he may mitigate his guilt by entering a protest and by advocating amendment, but he cannot completely absolve himself of guilt [except?] by disassociation. In the case of non-voluntary organizations, such as the state, the possibility of disassociation does not exist, and however much one may denounce the policies and programs of the government, one is inescapably involved in the common guilt. What is to be observed, however, is that the guilt rests upon individuals. Each shall be judged according to the measure of his involvement and responsibility. It is not "the state" that will be punished, but the individuals constituting the state.[30]

It seems to me that if we were to deny the truth of this, we should have to brace ourselves for a pastoral, liturgical and ethical revolution. Pastorally, we should have to find a reply to the elderly lady who said, "Our minister is such a nice young man, but he will keep blaming everything that happens in South Africa on me!" To seek to engender unwarranted guilt feelings is a most damaging pursuit, and it is not one confined to overtly Christian circles. Thus, for example, Mr. Julian Barnes writes in his television column about the enquiry of the "investigative" John Pilger into the plight of Australian aborigines in these terms:

> Pilger unrolled his grim history of slaughter, land-theft and discrimination in his usual telling way: that's to say, by making the viewer feel incredibly guilty about things he has no control over. You may not even have been to Australia, but when Pilger fixes you with his basilisk eye and tells you that many years

ago 'the billabongs ran with blood,' you know that the footprints found beside
the billabong exactly match your shoe size.[31]

Liturgically, the question will be, What are we doing when we invite people to
confess sins which they cannot feel responsible for having committed? Will this not
lead to unreality in worship? In what sense can someone else's particular sin be my
sin? How can I confess the sin of another? The concept of collective responsibility
should neither encourage us to confess actions which we did not perform nor provide
an escape route for excusing those sins which we did commit.

But, to repeat, the underlying difficulty is ethical. Have we done morality a service
if we appear to say that A can be held morally responsible for the evil B did and hence
be deemed guilty? Can we properly say that X is morally responsible for what Y did
even before X was born? I do not think that morality is served along those lines.

 IV

The second issue which arises from the Resolution on Racism and South Africa
is that of the role of churchly bodies in ethical matters. On what grounds do such bodies
make ethical pronouncements at all? Can they do this with integrity with regard to the
gospel of *agape* which, after all, should be their main concern? I do not think that it
should take us too long to answer this question.

If it is true that the Christian Gospel has to do with the whole of life, and not only
with some immaterial entity, the soul, which we tend on Sundays and neglect for the
other six days, then clearly we cannot exclude ethical concerns from Christianity. They
are, as I have said, integral to the Gospel. We are to love as we have been loved; and
among the signs of the Kingdom are that "the blind recover their sight, the lame walk,
the lepers are made clean, the deaf hear, the dead are raised to life, the poor are hearing
the good news."[32] It is easy to see that the Christian Gospel places a socio-ethical
demand upon those who receive it; and since, in our time, politics and government are
the means whereby human needs are met — or are not met — Christians cannot be
concerned with those spheres.

Indeed, this is so much taken for granted by many Christians today that any
cautionary words on the subject may appear to be issuing from Antichrist! I am told
that in some circles, the activists are jamming the agendas, and are utterly persuaded
that this is the right thing to do. Not indeed that the "disease of resolution" is altogether
new. In 1876 the celebrated Dr. Joseph Parker addressed the Assembly of the
Congregational Union of England and Wales in this way:

> What an amazing amount of so-called 'business' we have to do! We have to
> disestablish the Church [of England], modernize the Universities, rectify the

policy of School Boards, clear the way to burial-grounds, subsidize magazines, sell hymn-books, play the hose upon [the Anglican] Convocation, and generally give everybody to understand that if we have not yet assailed or defended them, it is not for want of will, but merely for want of time.

For good measure Parker hoped that it would soon be possible to reduce the Assembly's agenda to one sentence: "The usual speeches will be delivered by the usual speakers."[33] It may be that many church assembly habitués will feel a certain sympathy with Joseph Parker.

We can become so accustomed to our sheets of assembly resolutions that we never think of asking the question whether the socio-ethical implications of the Gospel require that we pronounce upon every conceivable issue of the day. Let us break the question into parts, and consider each part in turn.

First, is it possible for a churchly body to formulate a non-platitudinous position on an ethical issue? Here we stumble, in the wake of John C. Bennett, upon what are variously known as intermediate norms or middle axioms. A middle axiom is a proposition which is not so general and vague that all may agree with it and then do nothing about it; nor yet so detailed and technically specific that those who receive the resolution in which it is embodied can say, "The Church is not sufficiently expert in these matters to be giving specific advice of this kind, and we can therefore safely ignore this resolution." Let me attempt an illustration. A resolution to the effect that "We urge the government to strive for full employment" would probably command widespread support, and lead to no action. It is platitudinous. On the other hand, a resolution to the effect that "We urge the government to establish ten new Northumberland pipes factories on Tyneside with a view to combating unemployment in that area" would almost certainly be rejected on the ground that the churchly body perpetrating it is insufficiently competent in the economic, marketing and demographic circumstances of the region to resolve in those terms. A middle axiom might be that "We request the government, as a matter of urgency, to undertake a study to determine the types of industry best suited to Tyneside, and to investigate ways and means of establishing such concerns in the region." This is not a platitude — it asks a government to do something specific; neither is it so technically detailed as to risk rejection on the ground of the incompetence of the Church to deal with such matters. Moreover, the recipients of the resolution can be pursued from time to time to see how far they have got with the requested investigation, and their eventual findings can be reviewed and commented upon. Thus, non-platitudinous socio-ethical resolutions are not in principle impossible to draft.

But the second part of the general question is this: can a churchly body frame a motion which is truly representative of its often diverse and geographically scattered constituency? I believe that the answer is, sometimes it can, sometimes it cannot. The "Resolution on Racism and South Africa" commended considerable assent around the world and, moreover, its recommendations were quite specific. To the extent that it succeeded, it was successful because a large number of people felt that you cannot forever proclaim a Gospel which unites all sorts and conditions of people in God's *agape*, while at the same time, for example, tolerating a Lord's table divided along racial lines.

I do not think that it will always be practical to seek such a degree of unity on specific issues. Indeed, it is likely that the more geographically spread and culturally diverse the constituency is, the more difficult it will be to propose universally acceptable motions. There is some evidence to suggest that if a church council proclaims a socio-ethical view which does not represent the views of large numbers of its members, we have strain and stress in the family of Christ. How far could we say that a council's resolution represented the mind of the church, if we knew that its terms were hotly disputed by many church members? This is by no means a politico-organizational matter only. Fundamentally it is a theological question. For we cannot deny that God the Holy Spirit may address his people in a local church. Neither can we deny that the same God may address his people in a wider representative gathering. If we rule out the possibility that a God of truth could speak with a forked tongue, we can only conclude that in a situation in which the wider council's view contradicts that of the local church, either or both of the parties is insufficiently informed on the subject, or has been motivated by dubious objectives, or has not been listening carefully to God. This argues for some mutuality of oversight to be built into church structures as between the local and the wider groups; it argues for appropriate restraint on the part of the avant-garde, who may see themselves as leaders or prophets, and may indeed be called to leadership and prophecy, but who cannot lead if the troops are marching in another direction, and cannot prophesy if nobody is within earshot. Listen to these wise words of Robert Paul:

> Let us be honest, how far are the ethical concerns that occupy the churches today genuine concerns of the members, or to what extent are they sponsored by those who have a cold and calculating eye on the new trends of this age? I ask to be informed — I do not imply a judgment.[34]

I suggest that there are times when we should not so much be pressing for resolutions as engaging in detailed study, so that individual Christians and local churches may be well grounded in the Biblical principles and empirical factors which bear on those issues requiring gospel-based decision and action. If this suggestion is not heeded, and if interest groups persist in being determined in a resolution-orientated way, we may find that the old sectarianisms which centre in divergent understandings of ministry and sacraments pale into insignificance before the newer sectarianisms which will arise over ethical issues. When we reach a position of appearing to say, "Unless you agree with me on this ethical position, or on this socio-political platform, you are not a *bona fide* Christian and I shall have no further dealings with you," we have adopted an inherently sectarian stance, ironically, in the name of a uniting *agape*.

Church division then threatens, and the gospel of grace has been turned into a new legalism. That such legalisms can issue as easily from the so-called left wing as from the so-called right wing clear to anyone who has paid even the slightest attention to the North American Christian scene of the past twelve years.

At this point someone may object: but did not the World Alliance of Reformed Churches adopt a sectarian stance in suspending two of its member churches? I do not think so. It is one thing to say, "We have both received God's gift of salvation but, *in the last resort*, we cannot stand with you on this question, and we urge you to mend your ways, which we think constitute a denial of the Gospel, in order that fellowship may be restored"; it is quite another thing to say as the *first* step: receiving God's gift means endorsing our specific set of programmes and policies on socio-ethical issues. This would be a new legalism; a turning of the gift into a specific set of demands; the erecting of particular stances into conditions of fellowship. Paul would call it a "new circumcision" (Galatians 1). This is an inherently sectarian stance, whereas the other is reluctantly and, at best, only temporarily separatist. The underlying question is, How far is honest difference of opinion on ethical matters tolerable within the Church? The answer, I believe, is until the Gospel of God's grace comes to be denied. In the muddy field of ethics, Christians should not too readily reach the conclusion that their fellows are denying the Gospel. Any such decisions should follow the most thorough heart-searching, discussion and prayer.

In concluding this section I draw your attention to some words of the Baptist theologian Arthur Dakin, which are well worth pondering:

Many will agree that of late years the atmosphere of Church life has tended to be depressing; life has seemed to be little else than a series of problems calling forth challenge after challenge with little real possibility of doing anything about it. The ethical earnestness, the fearless facing of ethical problems and the strong desire to find a solution to them — all that has been praiseworthy and we should be ill-served were we to lose it. But the general effect of it has been the presentation of Christianity as a continuous striving and toiling with faint prospect of success. The appeal has been to be up and doing, and there has been much criticism of conduct, and emphasis on failure, and at times even nagging. In a word, the atmosphere has been little more than that of an ethical society presenting an ideal and calling for a continuous painful effort to achieve it. Is it too much to say that a firm grasp of the essential nature of evangelical ethics would bring here a radical change? It would bring rather the atmosphere of present triumph; the atmosphere of joy in what God has already accomplished; the sense of achieved emancipation in the individual; and resources of spirit for the new life.[35]

The third matter arising from the "Resolution on Racism and South Africa" (though almost any socio-ethical issue would raise it) is encapsulated in the question, How far, and on what basis, may Christians stand with integrity alongside others on ethical issues? It is, after all, quite clear that many people of good will, and not Christians only, are opposed to apartheid. I think we have no alternative here but to introduce the traditional theory of natural law as an aspect of the doctrine of creation, and therefore as having to do with God's grace. We are not here concerned with law conceived *naturalistically*. For this reason some Christians prefer to speak of God's common (as distinct from his saving) grace, by which all people are blessed with life, a sense of obligation, and some capacity for good; and which restrains the worst evils of which lives alienated from God by sin might otherwise be capable.

No matter which term is used, the point is that part of what it means to be human is that (provided we are in possession of normal human faculties) we can recognize the existence of the moral order. We are aware of obligation. We know that some things are right, and others wrong; that the good is to be pursued and the evil avoided.

Let it be said at once that such a view by no means commands the assent of all. Indeed, the humanist Hector Hawton thinks that the undermining of such a doctrine has been a principal result of humanism. He writes,

Perhaps the most fundamental change of outlook to which Humanism has contributed is the weakening of belief in an absolute moral law. Those who hold that there is a law defining right and wrong, either discoverable by natural reason or divinely revealed, cannot admit any exceptions. The consequences of an act therefore have no bearing on its rightness. It is our duty to obey the law, come what may. Commonsense is affronted by the harshness of this attitude.[36]

It is arguable that by selecting for criticism an extreme version of the many-sided natural law theory, Mr. Hawton hardly plays fair. Even those who hold to the existence of an absolute moral law have often, in practice, found it necessary to admit that people do not always appraise the law aright, and they have supplemented the deliverances of natural law as they understand them with the examination of means and possible or likely consequences. In other words, they have permitted both deontological and teleological considerations to come into play.

It cannot easily be denied that natural law theory has had a checkered history. Concerning some older applications of the idea Daniel Day Williams once pointed out that the Roman Catholic Church "not only puts it authority behind the ultimate principles, but it treats very complicated and debatable deductions from these principles as if they had the same authority."[37] Furthermore, the Church "puts a legalistic restriction upon the freedom of the Christian conscience in dealing with the unpredictable and always problematical stuff of actual social existence."[38] This latter point was reinforced by Ronald Preston: "the very theology whose *raison d'être* was to deal with specific problems, proceeded by a deductive method of reasoning from the alleged self-evident deliverances of natural laws in a way which prevented it from dealing adequately with empirical data."[39]

This point is well taken by a number of contemporary Roman Catholic scholars. As soon after the Second Vatican Council as 1967 Fr. James Scull was able to say, "There is perhaps no area within contemporary Catholic life and theology undergoing renewal and reform to a greater degree than Catholic moral theology."[40] Under the impetus of the Council a succession of Roman Catholic writers, of whom Charles Curran is a conspicuous example, have probed natural law theory and its applications to good effect. During the same period a number of Protestant ethicists have investigated the topic afresh. Prominent among these is Paul Ramsey, who has rightly said that "any conception of the nature of man is so far a conception of the natural law."[41] The humanist H.L. Elvin would agree. He has advocated concerted action on the part of Christians and humanists; he thinks that such action can take place on the basis of a common agreement on what has been found to be good in human life, and in a manner consistent with the strategy that "when speaking with those outside a faith one speaks in terms of the natural law."[42]

Some theologians concur. Thus, for example, when discussing the ethical position of Emil Brunner, W.M. Horton wrote,

> I agree with Brunner that the present moral consensus of mankind is 'very limited in character,' reducing itself to the universal presence of *some* 'sense of right,' *some* distinction between right and wrong, 'wherever there are human beings,' plus a very small residue of agreement between rival and largely conflicting definitions of the meaning of right and wrong. But I believe that this universal moral sense can be brought to greater clarity, and this small agreement as to the meaning of right and wrong can be increased, by patient and persistent conference between the adherents of different ethical traditions, even those remote from each other.[43]

After all, as John Macquarrie argued in his book, *Three Issues in Ethics (1970)*: any type of Christian ethical theory which denies the existence of, or the worth of this common moral experience, whether on grounds of total depravity or any other, is courting difficulty not only in the field of ethics, but also with respect to the doctrine of our creation in the image of God. We are back to the autonomy of morals once more, and to the different perspectives which may be brought to bear upon ethical issues common to all. Let me offer an illustration.

It is surely preferable that a Christian and a humanist, or a member of another world religion, should both make a financial contribution to a cause dedicated to the relief of the hungry millions in the world, than that either or both of them should withhold support on the ground that he cannot accept the overall world view of the other. Indeed, to an observer innocent of their world views their actual actions would appear to be very much the same. They would both write a cheque, or place money into a collection box; and the observer might well surmise (and, on the assumption that neither of the donors was a notorious hypocrite who liked to be thought well of, it would be legitimate so to surmise) that both parties share a common concern for the hungry, and a common desire to assist them. They share a motivation; they perform similar actions. The fact remains, however, that despite these important overlaps there will be areas of divergence too. If pressed, the Christian would admit as relevant motivations and areas of interpretation those which the other would exclude. Thus, in the course of his discussion of Butler's thought, my colleague Terence Penelhum has written: "the world-view of the believer differs from that of the unbeliever by *addition*. Throughout his writings Butler is clear that the view of human nature he himself holds is not one which *contrasts* with that of enlightened and reasonable secular men of his own day, but is one which broadens and deepens it, and can therefore be presented as a plausible extension of it."[44]

It is precisely as they present the extensions that Christians witness to their faith. If they are silent as to the extensions, they are shelving their responsibility of witnessing and as Robert McAfee Brown bluntly declared, "the minute we Christians begin to *sound* just like everyone else, we've lost the ball game."[45] Hence, for example, the concern expressed by the Mennonite political scientist, John H. Redekop, that the connection between what Mennonites do when they work for peace, and what they believe is not always clear. He writes that Mennonites

> stress that through the atonement Christ made possible forgiveness and salvation for all who believe. Those who accept this gift in faith have total peace *with* God. Through the Holy Spirit believers also then experience the peace *of* God. Because we are concerned about the well-being of others, including non-Christians, such recreated disciples of the Prince of Peace also seek peace *among* men. We seek to reduce, even eliminate, hatred and strife and war among all people.

> That's the official position. Sometimes it gets distorted....

> I have met some people who seem to believe that acceptance of the anabaptist peace position means that we should concentrate on getting governments to be less warlike. For these people, often zealous activists, the peace agenda includes pressure to achieve the following: less military research, [etc. etc.]...

I believe that our anabaptist peace position means that first we stress peace with God and then we stress a life exuding peace...Since we follow the way of peace we do not kill or otherwise violate the dignity and worth of human beings. One consequence of holding this view — but it is not the essence of the view — is that we encourage non-Christians, including governments, to stop killing one another and to stop making plans to do.[46]

Thus, for all that we may properly allow to natural morality, Christians will wish to acknowledge the reality, and the motivation derived from, God's holy *agape*. We neither wish to substitute an absolutely different morality for the existing natural morality; nor do we wish to prize natural morality away from the non-Christian by annexation. The moral is the moral whoever is looking at it; but for Christians the Gospel sharpens, deepens, personalizes, redeems, and revises the context of what is there in the moral. "Christian morality," wrote N.H.G. Robinson, "reaffirms *and* redeems the natural morality of men."[47]

If, finally, we ask, What is the context of Christian ethical thought and activity? we find that we have come full circle. For the context within which Christians live is defined by that redeeming, victorious *agape* which is focussed in the Cross.

From the Cross Christians draw their motives and attitudes, and also their courage and hope. To quote my revered teacher T.W. Manson:

The living Christ still has two hands, one to point the way, and the other held out to help us along. So the Christian ideal lies before us, not as a remote and austere mountain peak, an ethical Everest which we must scale by our own skill and endurance; but as a road on which we may walk with Christ as guide and friend. And we are assured, as we set out on the journey, that he is with us always, 'even unto the end of the world.'[48]

In those last words we have the eschatological note, which can never be erased from the Christian approach to ethics. The Christian's moral actions have a more than temporal significance, and to the extent that they are a reflection of God's *agape* it could hardly be otherwise; for *agape* is the hallmark of that Kingdom of which there is no end. No doubt a crude religious ethic of reward is offensive, not least to non-believing-naturally-morally-aware people. The fact remains that the Christian end of unimpeded, eternal fellowship with and service of God, though not a bribe, still less a *quid pro quo*, is a result and a fulfilment of that fellowship with God which even now we partially enjoy, and which, being grounded in victorious, atoning *agape*, can be broken by nothing, least of all by death.

NOTES

1. See Alan P.F. Sell, "Henry Grove: A Dissenter at the Parting of the Ways," *Enlightenment and Dissent*, IV (1985): 53–63.

2. H. Grove *A System of Moral Philosophy*, (London, 1749), I:3.

3. Romans 7:19.

4. Romans 7: 24–5.

5. See e.g. H.P. Owen, *The Moral Argument for the Existence of God* (London: Allen & Unwin), 1965.

6. Sydney Cave, *The Christian Way* (London: Nisbet, 1949), 132.

7. Quoted by S. Cave, op.cit., 157.

8. John Munsey Turner, *Conflict and Reconciliation. Studies in Methodism and Ecumenism in England 1740–1983*, (London: Epworth, 1985), 48.

9. See Matthew 15:7, 16:3; Mark 7:6; Luke 12:56.

10. G.F. Woods, *A Defence of Theological Ethics* (Cambridge: Cambridge University Press, 1966), 120.

11. See Donald G. Bloesch, *Freedom for Obedience* (San Francisco: Harper & Row, 1987); Oliver O'Donovan, *Resurrection and the Moral Order. An Outline for Evangelical Ethics* (Leicester: Inter-Varsity Press, 1986).

12. At certain points in the next section and in the last I shall draw upon my published articles: "*Agape*, Atonement and Christian Ethics," *The Downside Review* XCI (April 1973): 83–100; and "Christians, Humanists and Common Ground," *Journal of Moral Education* I (3, June 1972): 177–185.

13. C.K. Barrett, *The Gospel according to St. John* (London: SPCK, 1955), 180.

14. Romans 5:8.

15. W. Temple, *Readings in St. John's Gospel* (1945; reprint, London: Macmillan, 1955), 48.

16. Romans 8:39.

17. Romans 6:10.

18. R. Mackintosh, "The Fact of the Atonement," *The Expository Times* XIV (1902–3): 347.

19. T. Watson, *A Divine Cordial* (1663; reprint, Grand Rapids: Sovereign Grace Publications, 1971), 49.

20. John 13:34; 15:12.

21. C.H. Dodd, *Gospel and Law* (Cambridge: Cambridge University Press, 1951), 42.

22. See T.W. Manson, *Ethics and the Gospel* (London: SCM Press, 1960), 60–62.

23. W. Temple, op.cit., 223.

24. E.P. Dickie, *Revelation and Response* (Edinburgh: T. & T. Clark, 1938), 64.

25. For the full text of the Resolution see *Ottawa 1982. Proceedings of the 21st General Council of the World Alliance of Reformed Churches (Presbyterian and Congregational)*, ed. Edmond Perret (Geneva: World Alliance of Reformed Churches, 1983), 176–180. Some have felt that it was wrong to allow more than twenty years to elapse before the Alliance took action. But (a) it was right to give every opportunity for a change of heart, and (b) a body, such as the Alliance, whose resolutions are not legally binding on member churches, can carry conviction only if its deliberations are widely supported. An ecumenist of long experience has said that if you wish the world's churches to unite upon an issue, you must introduce the topic at least ten years before you need the decision.

26. Ibid., 177.

27. John Donne, *Devotions*, XVII.

28. Aristotle, *Nic.Eth.*, trans. and ed. Sir David Ross (London: Oxford University Press, 1954), 48.

29. J.H. Muirhead, *Elements of Ethics* (London: John Murray, 1982).

30. H. Stob, "Ethics: With What does it Deal?" *Calvin Theological Journal* XI (1, April 1976): 39. Reprinted, idem, *Ethical Reflections* (Grand Rapids: Eerdmans, 1978), 11.

31. Julian Barnes, *The* [London] *Observer*, 26 May 1985, 24.

32. Matthew 11:5.

33. Quoted by Albert Peel, *These Hundred Years. A History of the Congregational Union of England and Wales* (London: Congregational Union of England and Wales, 1931), 264.

34. Robert S. Paul, *Ministry* (Grand Rapids: Eerdmans, 1965), 184.

35. Arthur Dakin, "Evangelical Ethics," in *Studies in History and Religion*, ed. Ernest A. Payne (London: Lutterworth, 1942), 204–5.

36. Hector Hawton, "The Contribution of Humanism," *Aspects of Education*, July 1964, 56.

37. D.D. Williams, *Interpreting Theology 1918–52* (London: SCM Press, 1953), 74.

38. Ibid.

39. R.H. Preston, "The Study of Christian Ethics," *Theology* LXVII (1964): 146.

40. J.P. Scull, "Roman Catholic Moral Theology (Contemporary)," *The Dictionary of Christian Ethics*, ed. J. Macquarrie (London: SCM Press, 1967), 302.

41. Paul Ramsey, *Nine Modern Moralists*, (Englewood Cliffs, N.J.: Prentice Hall, 1962), 112.

42. H.L. Elvin, "The Standpoint of the Secular Humanist," in *Religious Education 1944–1984*, ed. A. Wedderspoon (London: Allen & Unwin, 1966), 184.

43. W.M. Horton, "Ethics for Today in the Light of the Protestant Religion," *The Congregational Quarterly*, January 1957, quoted by H. Cunliffe Jones, *Christ and Mission* (London: Independent Press, 1957), 10.

44. Terence Penelhum, *Butler* (London: Routledge & Kegan Paul, 1985), 126–7.

45. R. McAfee Brown, "Discoveries and Dangers," *New Christian*, 2 April 1970, 13.

46. John H. Redekop, "Peace and the M[ennonite] C[onference] [of] C[anada], *Mennonite Brethren Herald*, 18 March 1988, 70. Cf. idem., ibid., 15 April 1988, 12.

47. N.H.G. Robinson, *The Groundwork of Christian Ethics* (London: Collins, 1971), 305.

48. T.W. Manson, *Ethics and the Gospel*, 68. In a full discussion the doctrine of God the Holy Spirit might well be introduced at this point, for by the Spirit we are regenerated, renewed, and sustained in the Christian life. See Keith Ward, "Christian Ethics and the Being of God," *Scottish Journal of Theology* XXII (no. 1, March 1969): 78–89, especially page 89.

ECCLESIASTICAL INTEGRITY

 IV

ECCLESIASTICAL INTEGRITY

There are many ways of approaching the problem which underlies this intriguing and slippery title. My way is to invite you to imagine two piles of volumes of systematic theology. The section of ecclesiology in any of the volumes of the first pile will include some such sentence as this: "The unity, holiness and perfection of the Church are given in the creation of the Church by God, and they cannot be obliterated or marred." This is an affirmation of the Church's integrity, where integrity is understood — as the dictionary permits — as wholeness. In any of the volumes from the second pile of systematic theologies we may read something along these lines: "The quest of the integrity of the Church is not for the Church's sake, but for the sake of the Gospel through which the Church is called into being, and to which it witnesses." Anyone writing such a sentence has in mind the dictionary definition of integrity as honesty.

The wholeness assertion does not necessarily admit the notion that the integrity of the Church requires to be striven for by the empirical Church: the integrity is divinely given. It is *real* in the Platonic sense, it is not to be achieved. The honesty approach appears to be more *realistic* in another sense of that ambiguous term. It looks with a critical eye at the empirical Church; it recognizes that the treasure of the Gospel is in an earthen vessel; and it appears, prima facie, that along honesty lines we may more readily admit the notion of ecclesiastical failure: the quest is on, and we do not always succeed.

Matters are not quite that simple, however, for those who take the honesty path will normally wish to agree with their wholeness friends that it *does* make sense to say that the integrity, the wholeness of the Church is given: we neither create nor unify the

Church. As good honesty people they then concentrate upon the reality to hand, while resorting to eschatological "nows" and "not yets" as far as manifested wholeness is concerned. On the other hand, those who espouse the wholeness position cannot overlook what would happen to an impartial observer as the failures of the empirical Church. Accordingly, they have to redefine "empirical Church" so that the less attractive observed features of the institution are not deemed to belong to the Church at all. Thus, when at the 1985 conference of the Fellowship of St. Alban and St. Sergius Hugh Whybrew suggested that the Orthodox emphasis upon the holiness of the Church has reference more to the ideal than to the empirical Church, "This raised considerable controversy, for it touched on a basic divergence which is in fact concerned less with reality *versus* the ideal, than with differing perceptions of what elements of the empirical Church constitute the reality of the Church as opposed to incidental phenomena."[1] This explanation would seem to *concede* Mr. Whybrew's point, for if it is possible for one empirical phenomenon to be discounted, why not all? In this way the empirical Church suffers death by evaporation through redefinition, and we are left with an ideal Church about which much can be said and little can be known.

The situation is still more perplexing when those who maintain the Church's integrity, its wholeness, do not have in mind only a Platonic Church but also a concrete reality in the world. For an example of the confrontation between asserters of ecclesiastical integrity in this sense and seekers after it, we may turn to the New Valamo Consultation report on "The ecumenical nature of the Orthodox Witness." Appended to the report are a number of comments by members of non-Orthodox Christian world communions. Among these is a contribution from then Mr., now Bishop, David E. Jenkins, who adverts to

> a fundamental difficulty about Orthodox statements about the Church. This is that on the face of it many of these statements seem plainly and as a matter of fact false. Or if they are not false then it is quite unclear what their meaning is. Thus the question about credibility arises because these ecclesiological statements seem to be unbelievable, either because facts so plainly contradict them or because it is difficult to understand what we are being asked to believe.

> Let me illustrate the problem from the Valamo report. We are told that "the Orthodox understand the Church in the light of the Eucharist". This leads to a great statement about the Church being placed both "in the very centre of history" and "at the end of history". We then have the important statement "The Church which has this eucharistic character is not an abstract or speculative idea but *a concrete reality*" (my underlining). It is here that the difficulties about either factual contradiction or unclarity of meaning begin. It seems significant that the statement continues "whenever the people of God are gathered together in a certain place" and cites "*epi to auto*" from I Cor. 11:20. But in the context of this verse Paul is making the point that when they

do come together they do *not* realise a *"kuriakon deipnon"* because of some defects in their intentions and behaviour. That is to say that at this primitive stage the Apostle is already having to deal with contradictions between "concrete reality" (certainly, concrete happenings) and what the Church (or the Sacraments) "really are". Statements straightforwardly and ontologically linking what the Church as a whole and as such lives by, symbolises and hopes for and what the church in any local situation "concretely is" seem either not to correspond to the facts (so that what the Church is claimed "concretely" to be it "concretely" is not) or else to have no clearly graspable meaning.[2]

Lest it be thought that the Orthodox alone merit adverse criticism in this connection, I hasten to quote a splendid example of godly vacuity from a Reformed writer. R.B. Kuiper asserts, sensibly enough, that recourse has been had to the concept of the invisible Church because "we cannot tell with certainty who have been regenerated and who are in an unregenerate state." Two pages later, however, he declares that "the visible church is glorious in so far as it resembles the invisible church." He proceeds to advise us that sometimes the visible church is but "a caricature of the invisible," sometimes the former feebly reflects the latter; but "there are also instances in which the visible church concertedly emulates the invisible."[3] Kuiper wisely refrains from specifying when such occasions occur, or what criteria he employs for determining the degree to which an empirical reality faithfully or otherwise reflects an invisible reality the constituents of which are, on his own hypothesis, unknown to us. Thus from all sides, some have come to the refuge of the invisible Church: the honesty party holding that the Church we *cannot* see, or cannot see yet, is the whole Church; the wholeness party asserting that much of the Church we *can* see is not *really* the Church at all.

The problem as thus far outlined has a long history. How can the Church be both the spotless and virgin bride of Christ and, concurrently, manifestly sinful, as honesty requires us to recognize? In the early centuries the matter came to a head when Augustine responded to the Donatists, who held that pure sacraments required a pure ministry. Augustine's reply to the effect that the efficacy of the sacraments is not determined by the character of the minister has caused concern in Orthodox circles from that day to this, for it seems to admit too easily the possibility of rotten apples in the Church's barrel. Among the more recent ways of dealing with the problem in the West has been the definition of papal infallibility. The empirical Church is perfect, whole, only on those rare occasions when one man speaks *ex cathedra*. It is well known that the Old Catholics are not alone in querying this way of solving the problem.

On occasion those who wish to maintain the actual integrity of the Church turn to the view that the Church is a prolongation, continuation, or extension of the Incarnation. As the body of the spotless lamb of God, the Church is whole — its integrity cannot be gainsaid. However, in view of the manifest failure and sin of the Church this is a very difficult position to maintain in respect of the empirical Church. If it refers only to the invisible Church then it is quite impossible to employ the model of

Incarnation, which includes the concept of material enfleshment. As to the empirical Church, P.T. Forsyth long ago fulminated against those who would define *it* as an extension of the Incarnation:

> It is regenerated human nature in which Christ dwells. But that cannot be a prolongation of His Incarnation, wherein there was no regeneration...That which owes itself to a rebirth cannot be the prolongation of the ever sinless.[4]

A further way of asserting the wholeness of the Church is by appealing to the antiquity and unchangeableness of the institution. That which has been handed down from the past is authoritative; and if, for example, certain practices should appear which have no obvious links with the past then the reasoning deployed — by Basil of Caesarea among others — is that the apostles did in fact authorize these practices, but secretly.[5] Where doctrine is concerned appeal is made to truth embryonically declared. Neither of these traditional responses has any more appeal to harder-nosed advocates of honesty than to those popular nineteenth-century Anglo-Catholic apologies which find a large part of their Church order in what Christ must *surely* have said to his apostles during those forty days between the resurrection and the ascension about which we are almost entirely ignorant.

As to unchangeableness as a sign of integrity: on this point Herbert Waddams found himself puzzled by the philosopher H.A. Hodges. Hodges had written, "This absence of change, which makes the Eastern Church appear to some in the West as lifeless and fossilised, nevertheless guarantees the identity of its faith and order with those of the undivided church."[6] To this Waddams replied, "An absence of change may betoken a complete break in identity, *if* the essence of the original is adaptation and relevance to the world of the day."[7]

The matter is even more complicated yet. For standing between our two piles of systematic theologies is a smaller collection of texts which owe something to both "wholeness" and "honesty" views. Bernard Lord Manning (referring to Congregationalists) recognizes both the propensity to failure of the empirical church, its physical inescapability, and its divine origin:

> The visible organized local church is for us the earthen vessel which carries the real presence of the Saviour. From this there has always followed among us a vigorous conscious churchmanship which refuses to acknowledge any superior or equal power on earth, which asserts its complete right to self-government and to self-discipline...On the one hand Congregationalists have outdone all other Christians in the emphasis that they have laid on the visible church and on the supreme importance of continuous personal exercise in it by every individual. On the other hand Congregationalists have clearly understood, frankly confessed, and effectually lived by the truth that this

all-important visible church is a divine spiritual society, not an earthly historic society, that it depends wholly on grace, not at all on law.[8]

What is striking here is the declaration that the empirical Church *is* even now the whole Church, for it comprises the saints — those called out of the world and gathered under the gospel. Writers in this tradition have learned their ecclesiology from Robert Browne, John Owen and others, and the more recent ones among them have concurred with John Whale, who said that "it would be an Irish result if the only discernible mark of the Church were its invisibility."[9] At the same time, however, their honesty has required them to admit that the saints are saints by name if not always by nature and practice, and that the churches are earthen vessels. They have thus been prompted into ecclesiastical discipline of a kind which at its worst has encouraged mutual "saint-watching" of a somewhat neurotic kind. Furthermore, and however it may be with the whole and *invisible* Church, the wholeness of the empirical Church has frequently been shattered by the honesty of its members, so that one person's integrity has been another person's secessionist tendency.

Some years ago John Huxtable contrasted the integrity, wholeness, of the gathered company of saints with the impression he had received from Anglicans concerning their Church:

> When Anglicans talk of the Church they almost always give the impression of meaning the hierarchy and the priesthood, almost as if the laity were little more than a necessary background to the labours of bishop, priest and deacon. This is particularly striking to a Congregationalist, for whom the local Church is a whole after a fashion in which, apparently, the parish church is not. A Congregational minister and his people are so closely knit that he cannot function without them; and this is an indication of the belief that Church acts are indeed acts of the Church and not simply of Church officials: the Church, *not the minister*, celebrates the Eucharist.
>
> This is epitomised in the Church Meeting, that characteristic feature of Congregationalism.[10]

Once again, however, integrity, honesty, prompts the remark that Church Meetings can degenerate into democratic assemblies in which majority rule is the order of the day rather than gatherings of saints all seeking unanimity in Christ. And as for the ideal equality of pastor and people — it has not always been realized. There have been autocrats and bullies, and there was the prince of the pulpit who disgraced himself in my view with a one-sentence reply on a post card to a village church which had invited him to preach the anniversary sermon. The prince replied, "Can an eagle sit on a sparrow's nest?"

In attempting to adjust myself to the twists and turns I have described, I come to the conclusion that the Church's integrity, its wholeness, is given by God and that its complete manifestation is a matter for the *eschaton*. It *makes sense* to speak of the invisible church which is know to God alone, but *we* have to deal with the sometimes all-too-visible Church if, as I believe, being in fellowship is part of the definition of Christian. Accordingly, those who are saints by calling will do well to seek that ecclesiastical honesty which is consonant with the Gospel by which they have been claimed. In this quest they will certainly fail. They may even shatter the *empirical* wholeness of the Church either because of failure or because of their honesty. Standing in the line of Dissenting martyrs as I do, I cannot but assert that there have been times in Church history when it was more right, so to speak, to break a hypocritical empirical institutional unity than to maintain it. But such an assertion should always be made with real regret; secession should always be a last resort; deciding whether or not to secede is a complex question, and one which has sometimes received an over-prompt answer. The fact remains that it is a broken empirical body that we see.

I should like to add one qualification to what I have said concerning the relation-ship between empirical wholeness and honesty. Under political or religious systems which deny human rights it sometimes happens that a *lack* of integrity in the sense of honesty, far from hindering the empirical unity or integrity of the Church may actually be the only thing which will preserve that unity. That is to say, strictly dishonest statements are made by Christians with a view to preserving the empirical wholeness of the Church. The contexts to which I am referring are those in which we have what Sir David Ross would have called a clash of prima facie duties: on the one hand the duty to be honest and tell the truth; on the other, the duty to do all in one's power to secure the Church's visible unity and the preservation of its actual fellowship. Nothing I say concerning the importance of honesty is to be taken as implying adverse judgments upon Christians who are called upon to make difficult choices of the kind just described; choices of a kind we, in our society, are not disturbed by.

What are some of the areas in which honesty should be striven for in the hope that the given wholeness of the Church may more nearly be manifest? I should like to offer some reflections on confessional integrity and ecclesiological integrity.

Confessional integrity

In Lutheran circles the Augsburg Confession of 1530 is viewed as a witness to the wholeness of the communion. By contrast, the Reformed family (Reformed, Pres-byterian and Congregational) has no single confessional statement to which all adhere. In the sixteenth century more than sixty Reformed confessions were drawn up,[11] and in the last thirty years more than thirty declarations and statements have been devised by Reformed Churches.[12] Though more reluctant to *use* the statements they devised, the Congregationalists were ever willing to declare the faith commonly held among them, as witness Williston Walker's *The Creeds and Platforms of Congregationalism* (1893), which covers more than six hundred pages and whose last item is dated 1883. It is true that in the early years of the World Presbyterian Alliance (1875)[13] the possibility of drawing up a confession of faith for the whole family was seriously considered on two separate occasions.[14] The matter was eventually shelved, however, partly because it became clear that an agreed form of words would forever elude the members, and partly because of the realization that the Alliance was a fellowship of churches, and not itself a Church. The current Constitution of the Alliance invokes the word "ethos," and includes the following paragraph:

> Any Church which accepts Jesus Christ as Lord and Saviour; holds the Word of God given in the Scriptures of the Old and New Testaments to be the supreme authority in matters of faith and life; acknowledges the need for the continuing reformation of the Church catholic; whose position in faith and evangelism is in general agreement with that of the historic Reformed confessions, recognizing that the Reformed tradition is a biblical, evangelical and doctrinal ethos, rather than any narrow and exclusive definition of faith and order, shall be eligible for membership.[15]

However it may be with the confessional integrity of the family as a whole there can be no denying that a Christian communion as replete (some would say as littered) with confessions as the Reformed is well placed to illustrate the problems of confessional honesty.

Professor Fred H. Klooster has written that "to remove the binding character of the confession...would...mean the end of a confessional church."[16] but if confessions are acts of confess*ing*, then to be bound to past confessions is to court the difficulty which Waddams detected in Hodge's remark concerning the Orthodox: the possibility of contextual adaptability under the Spirit may appear to be ruled out.

Moreover, it cannot be denied that the classical creeds do pose problems of commission and omission to those who would confess the faith with integrity today. For example, the First and Second Helvetic Confessions and the Belgic Confession anathematize the Anabaptists. Most of us nowadays feel uncomfortable over this, and in current dialogue with the Mennonites, the heirs of the Anabaptists, the Reformed are trying to come to terms with this part of their history.[17] Again, the Westminster Confession's polemical references to the Pope were "bracketed" by the 1986 General Assembly of the Church of Scotland, but (for the moment at least) retained by the General Assembly of the Presbyterian Church in Ireland. So much for confessional commissions. As to omissions, one might justifiably suppose that a Church confessing the faith today would wish to speak more clearly than did the classical confessions on the doctrine of creation (which the earlier fathers did not have the capacity to devastate) and on witnessing in a pluralistic, economically and racially divided world. We might conclude that ecclesiastical confessional integrity is always *in practice* achieved only by modifying and supplementing the confessions of the past.

Quite apart from classical confessional commissions which make us uncomfortable and omissions which we have to make good, the presuppositions of the older confessions cannot go unchallenged. In particular, we cannot pretend that modern biblical criticism has not arrived. We cannot rest easy with the proof-texting by which many classical confessional doctrinal statements are supported. Nearly one hundred years ago, and with characteristic wit, that self-styled refugee from confessional Calvinism, Robert Mackintosh, wrote of what was

> perhaps the most marvellous statement in the whole [Westminster] Confession — that Scripture is 'not manifold.' Doubtless, to the dogmatist, peering about everywhere for proof-texts, the differences have no meaning. Hill, valley, and plain, cliff and waterfall, are nothing to the man with the muck rake. Assuredly, what one sees depends on the observer even more than on the object. But the Confessional use of proof-texts is even more precious and beautiful than the Confessional affirmations about them. That an oath cannot oblige to sin is proved by the example [?] of David in his relations with Nabal and Abigail. The 'contingency of second causes' is proved by a man 'drawing a bow at a venture,' or by the occurrence of a fatal accident when an axehead 'lights' on a bystander. Difficult questions on the doctrine of Providence are settled by the story of David and the men of Keilah. Finally — and I specially recommend this to the admirers of the Establishment principle — the proof that the civil magistrate may lawfully summon religious synods is found in the fact that Herod consulted the chief priests in order to plot more successfully how to murder the infant Jesus. Comment on these citations could be nothing but a feeble anti-climax. Let us treasure them up in our hearts.[18]

We cannot nowadays take the proof-texting way; but the question as to how our contemporary confessing is to be related to the Bible understood as the supreme rule of faith and life is by no means resolved.

What is not always recognized by the ardently confession-minded is that the authors of the confessions themselves often invited guidance in their prefaces. Such a request as that penned by the writers of the Scots Confession (1560) runs like a refrain through many more. They protest "that if any man will note in our Confession any chapter or sentence contrary to God's Holy Word, that it would please him of his gentleness and for Christian charity's sake to inform us of it in writing; and we, upon our honour, do promise him that by God's grace we shall give him satisfaction from the mouth of God, that is, from Holy Scripture, or else we shall alter whatever he can prove to be wrong."[19] In a word, the compilers of confessions knew that their work was to devise standards, or frame declarations, which would be *subordinate* to

Scripture, and hence revisable to the extent that they did not faithfully *interpret* Scripture.

Evidence that the removal of a *binding* confession need not mean the end of a confessing Church in an orthodox sense is, ironically, provided from within the Reformed family itself. It is striking that the eighteenth-century English Congregationalists remained for the most part orthodox (i.e. trinitarian) while the English Presbyterians, despite the Westminster Confession, became for the most part unitarian.[20]

It is further of importance to note that in the same century those who refused to *subscribe* at Salters' Hall (1719) nevertheless professed their trinitarian orthodoxy: we "freely declare, that we utterly disown the *Arian* Doctrine, and sincerely believe the doctrine of the blessed Trinity, and the proper Divinity of our Lord Jesus Christ." As if in anticipation of a *tu quoque* they point out in a footnote that "The human words...are used only to notify the things we speak of"[21] For them churchly integrity meant not subscribing to the words of men, but cleaving only to the Word of God. The Dissenter Ebenezer Latham was of like mind, and he may speak for them all:

'Hereticks and schismaticks' in the modern use of words is but a sort of theological scare-crow, a kind of Billingsgate language in the Church...That remedy for division is worse than the disease; 'tis adding human explications, the words of men, to the words of God...All their frightful anathemas are but ecclesiastical puffs, they do no execution, their squibs and canons recoil on themselves; for they incur the guilt of this crime when they usurp the throne of Christ, make laws in his church, and substitute their own interpretations in the room of scripture itself, teaching for doctrines the commandments of men...As protestant dissenters, we are not tied down to any authoritative interpretations...and Christian people should encourage their ministers to the impartial examination and study of the originals.[22]

Perhaps we had better award points all round by saying that there can be integrity and lack of integrity both in subscribing and in not subscribing to confessional statements. The crucial matter, however, is integrity in confessing.

But the question presses: how can we know that acts of confessing have integrity? The only answer I can give will not satisfy those who seek precision tools. It may even strike them as lax in the extreme. I can only say that confessing has integrity when it arises from prayerful recourse to the God who, by the Spirit through the Scripture addresses his people in a fellowship which is real now and linked to the apostolic testimony of the ages. Our discernment is not infallible. Certainly in my own tradition where the words of Scripture have been exalted over against Spirit and fellowship crude fundamentalism has resulted; and when the Spirit's guidance has been privatized and claimed apart from the Bible and the fellowship, we have been encumbered with the private mysticisms or gnosticisms of individuals. Again, there are ways of exalting the idea of fellowship which lead to difficulties, as Lovell Cocks pointed out long ago:

> The truth is that the warm informality and ready sympathies of the fellowship have often proved even more disastrous to the Church than dogmatic rigidity and institutional legalism. The danger threatening the institution is that outward observance will be substituted for inward surrender. But the besetting sin of the fellowship is that harmony will be preferred to holiness, popularity to principle, and unanimous resolutions to obedience to the Word of God.[23]

The quest of honesty entails the holding together of Spirit, Word and fellowship (tradition included), and all in subservience to the good news of God's grace in Christ. If we once move to the position of appearing to say that salvation is by Christ *plus* confessional *subscription* then we have landed in a version of the Galatian heresy — and one of a most Pelagian kind. This possibility is ever before my own tradition (I do not presume to speak of others) and, what is more, it is a pitfall which is wider and deeper than might be supposed. It need not be overtly a matter of confessions as such. Sometimes the impression has been given from Reformed pulpits that salvation is by assent to the divinely revealed plan of salvation. This plan has been rehearsed in all its pre- and post-Adamic detail and the only satisfactory response to it has been pre-determined by the preacher. Salvation seems to depend on assent to the plan — a work indeed! Thus, if the most that a hearer can say is that "Jesus is my master and friend" he will be viewed askance (even denounced) as an old-fashioned liberal, perhaps even as a crypto-Unitarian. But the same Bible from which the alleged plan of salvation is deduced also contains sufficient pastoral advice on not giving strong meat to babes, for example. This suggests that a distinction must ever be drawn between the general proclamation of the Church as a whole — and certainly between an individual preacher's description of the divine plan — and what an individual church member may be expected to profess. Church members are sinners who have begun to respond to God's grace in Christ; the terms of fellowship may not be so amended that only card-carrying supralapsarians (or liberationists, or feminists or recipients of "second blessings" or those of any other new circumcision) need apply.

The quest of an honest confession of faith entails the holding together of Spirit, Word and fellowship — and all in subservience to the good news of God's grace in Christ.

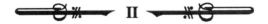

Ecclesiological integrity

Integrity in relation to the Gospel must also be our objective where ecclesiological matters are concerned. I think that this is the most important sentence in this lecture, but its analysis is not easy. Or, at least, there are real dangers in attempting to *define* the heart of the gospel, for our definitions themselves must be subject to the Gospel and not determine it. But what I have in mind is this: that God in grace, by the Spirit through the Word, calls out a people for his praise and service. Those thus called are the Church. But how are we to recognize the Church? It must have some bodily presence in the world if we take seriously the mission to which it is called. One reply has been to say that the Church may be recognized as such if its ministry is of a certain kind. Indeed, the wholeness of the Church depends upon its having, shall we say, a three-fold ministry in a historic succession. Such a ministry is sometimes said to be a sign of the Church's wholeness. Others, like the converted Dominican John Craig took a line which became strong in some Reformed circles. As bluntly as any he declared in his *Catechism* of 1581 that the signs or marks of the Church are "The Word, the Sacraments, and Discipline rightly used."[24] It is to be noted that at their best the proponents of such views do no regard either the ministry or the marks as the *definition* of the Church, but only as external evidences whereby the empirical Church may be located. It is a narrow path, however, and when some stumble all manner of questions of honesty are raised. At the present time these questions are raised especially in regard to the ministry and the sacraments, and on these I shall focus by way of illustration.

I should wish to side with P.T. Forsyth who, in an address delivered seventy years ago, said,

> In our view the unity of the Church is founded in the creative act of our moral redemption which creates our faith to-day and which created the Church at first; it is not in the traditional polity, creed, or cultus we inherit. If unity is in polity Christ died in vain. Unity is in the Gospel, it is not in orders nor sacraments, valuable as these are. The one is constitutive, the others but convenient.[25]

If this be true a number of things immediately follow.

First, we cannot honestly say that the Church depends for its being upon the ministry. This would be to place the ministry above the Gospel. Not surprisingly many Reformed churches have taken strong exception to the assertion in the so-called Lima document of the World Council of Churches *(Baptism, Eucharist and Ministry)* to the effect that the ordained ministry "is constitutive for *[sic]* the life and witness of the Church."[26] *A fortiori* we cannot say that the Church depends on a particular order of ministry. (On the other hand, we must take more seriously than some Reformed Christians have done God's use of means, and his relationship with the created order.) Here, I believe we have one of the crucial divides in (what remains of) Christendom. Dr. Kenneth Kirk still has his supporters. He wrote:

> If then we follow the teaching of Scripture and the tradition of the Church, we are bound to say that a valid ministry is one which, in accordance with primitive ordering, proceeds in due succession from the apostles by laying on of hands of the Essential Ministry; and that should such a ministry fail, the apostolic Church, which is the Body of Christ in space and time, would disappear with it (for the two are inextricably bound together), and the whole preaching of the Gospel message to the nations would be in the most urgent jeopardy. These things we do not say of non-episcopal ministries; for judged by scriptural and apostolic tests we find them to be invalid.[27]

These sentences bristle with puzzles which have been thoroughly treated in the past forty years. However it may be with tradition, Scripture does not make pronouncements on the validity of ministry in Kirk's sense of the term. Many have shown up the problems attaching to the historic succession, and T.W. Manson argued conclusively against Kirk that there was no handing-on of authority by the apostles of the kind required by Kirk's theory.[28]

Secondly, we cannot with integrity say that there is a case for re-ordination where the reconciliation of ministries is concerned. The point was classically put in the seventeenth century by John Howe to his friend Seth Ward, the Bishop of Exeter:

> Why, pray Sir, said the Bishop to him, what hurt is there in being twice Ordain'd? Hurt, my Lord, says Mr. Howe to him; the thought is shocking; it hurts my Understanding; it is an absurdity: For nothing can have two Beginnings. I am sure, said he, I am a Minister of Christ...and I can't begin again to be a Minister.[29]

Elsewhere Howe showed his awareness of the proximity of the Galatian heresy when he said "Without all controversy the main inlet of all the distractions, confusions, and divisions of the Christian world hath been by adding other conditions of Church communion than Christ hath done."[30] For all his antinomian tendencies, Tobias Crisp (1600–1643) drew the right conclusion: "so far as you set up any props unto Christ the foundation, that is to bear up all by Himself, so far you disparage Christ; so far you bring Him down, and give Him not the pre-eminence."[31]

At this point some, including many Anglicans, will be inclined to protest that my points are *passé*. They have learned the distinction between *esse* and *bene esse*, and are persuaded that episcopacy, as they conceive it, is of the *bene esse* of the Church, not of its *esse*. But then some of them sometimes behave as if it were otherwise! They feel most uneasy about *reciprocal* inter-communion although, as I understand it, there is nothing in canon law to prevent it; and in the Lima document, it is hard to see why the threefold ministry is so strongly urged upon us all when it is at the same time "increasingly recognised that a continuity in apostolic faith, worship and mission has been preserved in churches which have not retained the form of historic episcopate."[32] For many of us the apostolic succession is a matter of faithfulness to the apostles' Gospel; it is not a matter of particular ecclesiastical orders. In response to the Lima text's suggestion that non-episcopal churches ought to ask themselves whether they may not need to recover "the sign of episcopal succession,"[33] one Reformed church gently enquired, "of what is an heretical bishop a sign?"[34]

This leads us to the third consideration, and to the concept employed by Kirk: validity. Along the line I am pursuing it is not possible with integrity to speak of valid ministries, valid sacraments. These are meaningless locutions, if not blasphemous. The ministry is God's gift; the sacraments are his gifts; and it has always seemed ironical to me that among those most apt to invoke the category of mystery are some who are quickest to say "lo here" and "lo not there" where questions of validity are concerned. A collage of brief quotations from Bernard Manning will underline the point:

> The grace of God...needs no legal machinery to protect it...The Supper of the Lord is either celebrated or not celebrated. The Body and the Blood of Christ are spiritually received or they are not received. We simply do not know what an irregular or an invalid sacrament is. We do not deal in percentages with grace of God...When we can botanize about the Burning Bush, either it has ceased to burn or it has been consumed...We decline still, as we have always declined, to have episcopalian ordination of ministers...made into a sort of new circumcision within the limits of which alone is there the full and valid and regular operation of God's grace...As long as, and only as long as, episcopacy menaces the doctrine of free grace Congregationalists [and not only they] will be relentless about it.[35]

It will be said, of course, that Anglicans, at least, are not required to subscribe to a particular theory of apostolic succession.[36] Even Gabriel Hebert said this.[37] This only makes it harder for non-episcopalians to know what it is they are invited to take into their systems.

Furthermore, no matter what Anglican theologians may say upon the matter, it cannot be denied that the idea that ordination into one specific tradition alone suffices to validate sacraments is strongly entertained by some Anglicans at the grass roots. I call in evidence two contributions to the Letters page of the [Anglican] *Church Times* of 27 February 1981. At that time the possibility of a covenant between several English churches was under consideration (the result was in the end negative). With reference to this matter W.M. Davies writes: "If, under the covenant scheme, the Eucharist was celebrated by a non-episcopally ordained minister, the sacrament would be of doubtful validity. We cannot, of course, put limits on the mercy of Christ, but we should not presume on that mercy because we prefer our own man-made schemes to the ordinances of Christ's Church." Kathleen Blayney follows suit:

> Surely the *spiritual power* — nothing to do with magic — given to priests at their ordination to consecrate the eucharistic bread and wine and to absolve penitents is what the apostolic succession is all about?....

> No one would doubt that God's grace is given to a Nonconformist in receiving Communion according to his rite; but an Anglican like myself could not possibly receive it as the true sacrament of the Body and Blood of Christ.

I commend these writers for their honesty, and I shall not pause to analyze their statements in detail. I do not say that they are intentionally sectarian in spirit, though from my perspective — as you will be now realize — what they say sounds very much like the implicit advocacy to a "new circumcision" (cf. Galatians 1).

My fourth point is that if ministry is not to be set above the Gospel, neither are the sacraments. For, as the eminently quotable Manning also said, "The Christian rites grew out of the Good News; they were not incantations to conjure it up from a void."[38] For this reason I believe that our integrity *vis-à-vis* the gospel is at stake if we declare, as even the Anglican/Reformed dialogue report declares, that the *sacraments* are constitutive of the Church.[39] Rather the Church is constituted by the call of God by the Spirit through the word of the Gospel, and the sacraments, like the preaching, bear witness to that good news. It is because I prize the Gospel of the free grace of God, and not because I diminish the sacraments, that I stand with Richard Baxter, who wrote, "It is a dishonourable doctrine against God and Christianity to say that God layeth his love and man's salvation so much on a Ceremony, as to damn or deny an upright holy soul for want of it...The thing signified is necessary to salvation."[40] As Peter Lombard said long ago, "God is not bound by his sacraments."[41] For this reason one of the most important terms in the vocabulary of the ecclesiologist of integrity is the blessed word "normally." But, as with ministry, so with sacraments: those who wish to flee what they see as sacerdotalism must pay due attention to the relations of God and things material, lest they fall into deism.

That the questions of ministry and sacraments have been occasions of division between Christians cannot be gainsaid. They are by no means the only potential prompters of schism and secession though there is no need to rehearse others. Suffice it to say that however it may be with the integrity, the wholeness, of the invisible Church, that of the empirical Church as been sundered — and often because of the integrity, the honesty, of its members. It has, indeed, been maintained that the divisions of the empirical Church are sinful, but the concept of integrity under the Gospel makes this too simple an assertion. It would, of course be difficult to deny the possibility that human pride and lust for power have played their parts in secession movements, but only a cynic would suppose that all those who have given their lives for their ecclesiastical cause were possessed of the martyr complex. To repeat an earlier remark: there do seem to have been occasions in the life of the empirical Church on which it has been "more right" that the visible unity of that Church should be sundered than that a hypocritical wholeness should be maintained.

But when times passes, moods change, lessons are learned, then is the time for healing; and one of the ways of reading the ecumenical movement of this century is to say that it represents an honest effort towards realizing the wholeness of the empirical Church. In the healing of breaches, forms of words assume great importance and one of the standing challenges is to determine which compromises may be accepted with integrity and which may not. Perhaps Ian Henderson was ill-advised to make the universal remark that "ecumenical language is framed not to describe but to conceal ecumenical actions,"[42] but so wise an ecumenist as John Huxtable, while admitting that ambiguity is unavoidable "since human words and formulae are but frail attempts to describe and witness to what lies far beyond our grasp," nevertheless agreed that "the fault comes when words are used to disguise meaning when it is important to know what is being said with some precision."[43] Elsewhere he cited the draft of the once proposed service of Anglican-Methodist service of reconciliation as evidence of intolerable ambiguity:

> It rests on an uneasy compromise because a crucial issue has not been faced. What the Methodists have to offer the Anglicans is not unambiguously comparable with what the Anglicans have to offer the Methodists. Methodists do not question Anglican orders. At least some Anglicans question, or even deny, Methodist orders. How, it may be asked, can there be an adequate and sufficiently unambiguous mutual commissioning or ministerial reconciliation unless and until there is a more clearly accepted doctrine of the Church and of the ministry within it? Unless two doctrines of the ministry in question can be more clearly seen to be different but not mutually inconsistent ways of accepting a commonly held conviction, it is difficult to see how a satisfactory service can be arranged.[44]

We are left with the challenge of balancing two positions with integrity: on the one hand the great seventeenth-century ecumenist Richard Baxter pointed out that "the contentions between the Greek Church and the Roman, the Papists and the Protestants, the Lutherans and the Calvinists, have woefully hindered the kingdom of Christ."[45] On the other hand, the Dutch theologian Abraham Kuyper declared that "the easiest way to match two non-fitting cog wheels is to remove the teeth. To make the wheels fit each other by removing the teeth is undoubtedly a work of love, for now the wheels are perfectly matched; they seem to be of one piece. But the truth is lost — the wheels are no longer cog wheels."[46] However we may adjudicate matters, Matthew Henry's warning may stand: "the question bye and bye will not be — in what place, or what posture we worshipped God; but, did we worship in the spirit?"[47]

I conclude with two reflections. First, we have seen that the wholeness of the empirical Church is shattered by those who, on grounds of honesty, take a stand for or against the truth of confessional statements, and the necessity or desirability of particular ecclesiastical orders. These matters are by no means unimportant. But may we not have put too high a price on intellectual accord? I am by no means entering a plea for anti-intellectualism. I am not denying that those who at evangelistic rallies stand under a banner which proclaims "All one in Christ Jesus" and then *easily* return home to divided Lord's tables are a little ostrich-like. But is there no way of reflecting theologically upon the nature of Christian fellowship, which *is* given, and which we *do* experience both within and across denominational boundaries, without suggesting either that doctrinal and church order stances are unimportant, or that differences over them necessarily entail secession and fragmentation? In a threatened and a divided world what are the permissible degrees of tolerance within the Church?

Secondly, as I have pondered this challenging — even forbidding — theme over the months I have sometimes found myself asking why it is that ecclesiastical groups of great integrity (honesty) are so often angular, falsely pious, censorious, sectarian in spirit — none of which characteristics foster or witness to the wholeness of the Church. Rightly or wrongly, I have consoled myself with the old evangelical thought that, after all, the definition of Christian is not "person of absolute integrity" but "sinner saved"; and that ecclesiastical groups are composed of such. Because they are saved expectations should be high; because they are sinners expectations should be realistic. As P.T. Forsyth said long ago, "It is the wills of men, and not their views, that are the great obstacle to the Gospel, and the things most intractable."[48] The test of the honesty, and the source of the wholeness of the churches is the Gospel which can deal with wayward wills. It is a Gospel which can redeem the most abysmal of failures, even ecclesiastical ones.

NOTES

1. Anon, "The conference of 1985," *Sobernost* VIII (1, 1986): 81.

2. *The New Valamo Consultation. The Ecumenical Nature of the Orthodox Witness* (Geneva: World Council of Churches, 1977), 38–9.

3. R.B. Kuiper, *The Glorious Body of Christ* (1966; reprint, London: The Banner of Truth Trust, 1967), 27, 29, 30.

4. P.T. Forsyth, *The Church and the Sacraments* (1917; reprint, London: Independent Press, 1947), 82–3.

5. Basil of Caesarea, *De. Sp. Sancto* XXVII, 66.

6. H.A. Hodges, *Anglicanism and Orthodoxy. A Study in Dialectical Churchmanship* (London: SCM Press, 1955), quoted by Herbert Waddams, *Meeting the Orthodox Churches* (London: SCM Press, 1964), 110.

7. Herbert Waddams, op.cit., 114.

8. B.L. Manning, *Essays in Orthodox Dissent* (1939; reprint, London: Independent Press, 1953), 117, 164.

9. John Whale, *Christian Doctrine* (London: Collins Fontana, 1957), 134.

10. John Huxtable in his "Introduction" to John Owen, *The True Nature of a Gospel Church and its Government* (London: James Clarke, 1947), 15.

11. The major Reformed confessions are collected by A.C. Cochrane in *Reformed Confessions of the 16th Century* (Philadelphia: The Westminster Press, 1966).

12. See e.g. *Reformed Witness Today*, ed. Lukas Vischer (Bern: Evangelische Arbeitsstelle Oekumene Schweiz, 1982).

13. The World Presbyterian Alliance (1875) united with the International Congregational Council (1891) in 1970, to form the World Alliance of Reformed Churches (Presbyterian and Congregational).

14. See Marcel Pradervand, *A Century of Service. A Short History of the World Alliance of Reformed Churches* (Edinburgh: The Saint Andrew Press, 1975), 28,37,41,43,132.

15. *Constitution and By-laws*, amended 1982 (Geneva: World Alliance of Reformed Churches.

16. Fred H. Klooster, "Theology, Confession and the Church," in *Church and Theology in the Contemporary World* (Grand Rapids: Reformed Ecumenical Synod, 1977), 30.

17. See *Mennonites and Reformed in Dialogue* (Studies from the World Alliance of Reformed Churches no. 7) eds. H.G. vom Berg, H. Kossen, L. Miller and L. Vischer (Geneva: World Alliance of Reformed Churches, 1986).

18. R. Mackintosh, *The Obsoleteness of the Westminster Confession of Faith*, 48; bound with his *Essays Towards a New Theology* (Glasgow: Maclehose, 1899).

For the pungent, neglected, blower-away of ecumenical cobwebs see my *Robert Mackintosh: Theologian of Integrity* (Bern: Peter Lang, 1977).

19. A.C. Cochrane, op.cit., 165.

20. It was not legal to have a capital "U" until 1813. See further Alan P.F. Sell, "Confessing the Faith in English Congregationalism," *The Journal of the United Reformed Church History Society* IV (1988): 170–215.

21. See *An Authentic account of several things done and agreed upon by the Dissenting Ministers lately assembled at Salters Hall*, 1719.

22. Quoted by H. McLachlan, *Essays and Addresses* (Manchester: Manchester University Press, 1950), 158. That more recent Anglicans have had difficulties over subscribing to the Thirty-nine Articles is clear from the Archbishops Report on *Subscription and Assent to the 39 Articles* (London: SPCK, 1968), Ch.V.

23. H.F. Lovell Cocks, "The Gospel and the Church" in *Congregationalism Today*, ed. John Marsh (London: Independent Press, 1943), 33–4.

24. See *The School of Faith. The Catechisms of the Reformed Church*, ed. T.F. Torrance (London: James Clarke, 1959), 160.

25. P.T. Forsyth, *Congregationalism and Reunion* (London: Independent Press, 1952), 21–2.

26. *Baptism, Eucharist and Ministry* (Geneva: World Council of Churches 1982), 21. See further my "Some Reformed Responses to *Baptism, Eucharist and Ministry*," *The Reformed World* XXXIX (3, September 1986): 549–565.

27. *The Apostolic Ministry*, ed. Kenneth E. Kirk (London: Hodder & Stoughton, 1946), 40.

28. T.W. Manson, *The Church's Ministry* (London: Hodder & Stoughton, 1948), Ch.II.

29. Edmund Calamy, *Memoirs of the Life of the Late Rev. Mr. John Howe, M.A.*, 1724, 39.

30. Howe's *Works*, ed. Henry Rogers, V: 226.

31. From *Christ's Pre-eminence*, an edited reprint of two of Crisp's sermons, Sheffield: Zoar Publications c. 1975, 24.

32. *Baptism, Eucharist and Ministry*, 29.

33. *Baptism, Eucharist and Ministry*, 32. I do not, of course, deny the necessity of *episcope* in the church. I only query the elevation of one form of it above all others, and (apparently in some cases) even above the Gospel itself.

34. See Alan P.F. Sell, art.cit., at n. 26, 560.

35. Bernard Lord Manning, *Essays in Orthodox Dissent* (1939; reprint, London: Independent Press, 1953), 114, 116–117, 133, 170.

36. Cf. e.g. the *Report* of the Lambeth Conference (1920): "The acceptance of Episcopal Ordination in the future would not imply any particular theory as to its origin or character...").

37. A.G. Hebert, *Intercommunion* (London: SPK, 1928), 86. For recent Roman Catholic thought see John A. Gurrieri, "Sacramental Validity: Ecumenical Questions," *Ecumenical Trends* XV (5, May 1986): 69–73.

38. B.L. Manning, op.cit., 69.

39. See *God's Reign and Our Unity* (London: SPCK; Edinburgh: The Saint Andrew Press, 1984), 44 etc.

40. R. Baxter, *The True and Only Way of Concord*, 1680, 199.

41. P. Lombard, *Sententiae* IV. i. 4.

42. Ian Henderson, *Power Without Glory. A Study in Ecumenical Politics* (London: Hutchinson, 1967), 101.

43. John Huxtable, *A New Hope for Christian Unity* (Glasgow: Collins Fount Paperback, 1977), 46.

44. Idem, *Christian Unity: Some of the Issues* (London: Independent Press, 1966), 67.

45. R. Baxter, *Reliquiae Baxterianae* I. i.132, para. 26.

46. Quoted in *The Monthly Record of the Free Church of Scotland*, August 1968, 161.

47. J.B. Williams, *Memoirs of the Life, Character, and Writings of the Rev. Matthew Henry* (1828; reprint, Edinburgh: The Banner of Truth Trust, 1974), 182.

48. P.T. Forsyth, *Positive Preaching and the Modern Mind* (1907; reprint, London: Independent Press, 1964), 197.

THE INTEGRITY OF CHRISTIAN MISSION

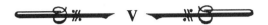

THE INTEGRITY OF CHRISTIAN MISSION

From some points of view this lecture would be better entitled, "Mission Muddles," or "Proclamatory Perplexities." The first verse of a missionary hymn by James McGranahan — still in use in some quarters — may explain why:

Far, far away in heathen darkness dwelling,
Millions of souls forever may be lost.
Who will go Salvation's story telling —
Looking to Jesus, counting not the cost?

Now, to make just one or two points per line: first, we may today feel properly uneasy about the absolutist reference to "heathen darkness." We know of the treasures of other civilizations and literatures; we cannot overlook the Christian doctrine of creation, which entails a revelation of God throughout the created order; and we cannot be entirely comfortable with the notion that all those needing to be missioned are "far, far away."

Secondly, the motive for missionary labour, that "Millions of souls forever may be lost" is, though urgent, not perhaps the noblest. By implication it casts aspersions upon the love of God, for it presupposes that people will be damned by not responding to the Gospel through no fault of their own. (If anything it is more likely that the Church will be damned for not telling the tidings.) Moreover, the motive of reaching the potentially damned is not an easy one to sustain in the West where, for so many, hell — as a theological commission reported in 1920 — has become "frozen over or turned to innocuous ashes."[1] Thirdly, the line "Who will go, salvation's story telling?" In our time there is, to say the least, a degree of confusion concerning the story to be told; and even if we knew precisely what we ought to say, we should soon meet Christians who would point out that it would not be quite decent for us to sally forth with the message — indeed, it would be an imperialistic and triumphalistic thing to do. Lastly, the pious phrase concerning "Looking unto Jesus, counting not the cost" rings a little hollow when we know that overseas workers of mainline churches have regular stipends, pensions, educational provision for their children, and a frequently higher standard of living than many, if not most, of those among whom they serve (and good reasons can be supplied for all of this); and when some in faith missions are so desperately counting the cost that their prayer letters home are phrased in ways which approximate to emotional blackmail: "This month we're praying in a new landrover. Will God fail us?"

It may not comfort us very much, but at least it will lend perspective to our enquiry if we recall that perplexity concerning mission is no new phenomenon. As early in the Christian era as the Acts of the Apostles we find Peter learning through his meeting with the Roman centurion, Cornelius, that the blessings of God are for Gentiles as well as for Jews.[2] For Peter this was a hard lesson. Calvin's successor in Geneva, Theodore Beza (1519–1605), maintained that there was no cause to take action on behalf of those far beyond the Church's borders, because the so-called Great Commission of Matthew 28 was deemed to have been fulfilled by the apostles. Beza held this position despite the fact that his own church had sent a mission to Brazil as early as 1557. By 1590, however, the Netherlander Adrian Saravia was found deploring the fact that "the apostolic zeal is now so chilled, that no one thinks of propagating the Gospel among the heathen."[3]

But discovery and trade were already taking a hand, and with the broadening of geographical and cultural horizons there developed a growing zeal for missions. In England and America this was a direct result of the Evangelical Awakening of the second half of the eighteenth century — though we should not overlook the extent to which the way had been prepared by the Society for the Propagation of the Gospel in New England (1649); by the refusal of such American settlers as Roger Williams the Baptist and John Eliot to believe that the Indians of the New World were "Canaanites" ripe for destruction; and by the vision of those Anglicans who founded the Society for the Propagation of the Gospel in Foreign Parts in 1701.

It is not without significance that the first of the modern missionary societies in Britain, that of the English Particular Baptists, was organized by ministers serving in, or close to, Doddridge's county, Northamptonshire; for Philip Doddridge (1702–57) was a leading advocate of missions. John Sutcliff of Olney, Andrew Fuller of Kettering — these and others — were instrumental in forming the Society. But the most ardent of all was William Carey, the cobbler cum schoolmaster cum preacher, of Moulton. What came to be called his Deathless Sermon, on Isaiah 54: 2–3, was preached at the Baptist Association meeting at Nottingham on 30 May 1792. Carey's theme was, "Expect great things from God; attempt great things for God." Some Baptists — prominent ministers among them — were more inclined to expect than to attempt. Their problem was theological. As I said, they were *Particular* Baptists; that is, they were Calvinists who believed that the elect of God alone would be saved, and that God alone could save them. By extension they arrived at the view that God would save his own in his own way, and in his own time, without the help of the likes of Carey and his friends. A delightful story concerning the elderly John Collett Ryland (which, sadly, cannot be authenticated) will make the point. It is said that when, at a meeting in Northampton, Carey urged the consideration of the missionary question, Ryland snapped, "Young man, sit down. You're an enthusiast."[4] As well as being a Calvinistic attitude, that was very much an educated eighteenth-century attitude as well. For many in that period looked back with horror upon the preceding century with its sectarian strife and its manifold enthusiasms, and they did not relish the prospect of a return of such phenomena. They would have endorsed Samuel Johnson's dictionary definition of enthusiasm: "A *vain* confidence of divine favour or communication" (my italics).

For all that, the tide was with Carey and his younger colleagues, and the Missionary Society was constituted on 2 October 1792. On 13 June 1793 Carey himself sailed for India under the society's auspices. Gradually, more and more came to see that even if God alone knew who the elect were, and even if he alone could save, this did not release Christians from the obligation to proclaim the Gospel to the ends of the earth.[5]

From the examples I have given you can see that there is nothing novel in hesitation concerning, or even opposition to, the missionary enterprise. In our own time we may specify a number of factors which combine to produce uncertainty concerning mission as such. First, one of the older motives to mission is now considerably weakened. There is no doubt that the perceived need to rescue the perishing before it was too late was a powerful spur in the past, and this motive is not entirely dormant yet. It is there in McGranahan's hymn from which I set out; and it is there in the kind of preaching on which many of the early missionaries were nurtured. A classical, and a chilling, example of this preaching (though not one typical of its author) is to be found in Jonathan Edwards' sermon entitled, "Sinners in the hands of an angry God": "The God that holds you over the pit of hell, much as one holds a spider, or some loathsome insect, over the fire, abhors you, and is dreadfully provoked...it is nothing but his hand that holds you from falling into the fire every moment. It is to be ascribed to nothing else that you did not go to hell last night."[6] Not surprisingly, some felt that they must go to the ends of the earth before other people's threads snapped.

I by no means minimize the compassion inherent is such missionary commitment: if you really felt that you had a message which would save those in grave danger of eternal damnation, it would, to say the least, be rather selfish to keep it to yourself. But there are three things to be said. First, the proclamation associated with this motive seems to begin from our sin, rather than from God's grace. No doubt we are needy sinners; but we really begin to see the truth of this only when we hear what God has done to save us. It was when Zacchaeus was in the presence of Jesus that he began to see who he was.[7] In my second lecture in this series I welcomed the way in which F.D. Maurice and John McLeod Campbell redressed theology's balance at this point. Secondly, I do not say that the idea of judgment is redundant. Whenever the Gospel is proclaimed we are judged insofar as we receive it or repudiate it. But this is to say that God's judgment is not upon a person's *future* state only. On the contrary, as P.T. Forsyth said,

> The judgment at the end of history is only the corollary of the judgment at the centre of history, and the close of that daily judgment in which we live...The mainspring of missions is not the judgment that *will fall*, but the judgment that *has fallen* in the Cross. It is not pity but faith, not so much pity for perishing heathen, but faith and zeal for Christ's crown rights set up for ever in the deed decisive for all the world. This is steadier than our views of the future, and it will carry our missions better.[8]

It follows, thirdly, that those who refuse to communicate the Gospel are under judgment, rather than those who, through no fault of their own, have never heard it. But again, the truest motive for mission is not our own security — if we do not tell others it will be the worse for us — but gratitude for what God in Christ has done. The motivation of Christian mission is identical with that of Christian ethics. In view of God's overflowing grace the Christian ought to say, with Paul, "it would be misery for me not to preach."[9]

Next, there is the perplexity prompted by the fact that some Christians who are supremely confident in their message seem to live in a pre-critical age, thereby denying the ongoing activity of the very Holy Spirit whom they claim as their inspiration. Other Christians are so confused as to what is to be proclaimed that they give themselves to good works, and become indistinguishable from any right-minded humanist; or else they devote themselves to method rather than to content — programming their computers to track down the existing membership of the Church, rather than proclaiming the Gospel to increase it. In this way they remove themselves ever further from their main task, though they are always busy. Thomas Torrance diagnosed the malady some forty years ago: "If Churches have lost their relevance it is because they have slackened their grip upon the Gospel of the Incarnation, Death and Resurrection of Christ, made easy and comfortable terms with the world, and only succeeded in neutralising the dynamic energy of faith."[10] Here is a strong plea that the Church's message is not to be uprooted from its anchorage in history,[11] and supremely in the Cross-Resurrection event. Indeed, P.T. Forsyth's dictum is worth pondering: "You may always measure the value to yourselves of Christ's Cross by your interest in missions."[12] Perhaps in these words there lies the explanation of the minister's lament. On the occasion of the twenty-fifth anniversary of his ordination, he said to his congregation, "Twenty-five years ago I though I was being ordained to be a fisher of men; but I find that I have become the keeper of an aquarium."

Yet again, even if some Western Christians know in principle what there is to be proclaimed, they are by no means at all certain that they ought to launch forth, or support those who do. They are burdened by racial guilt. We were the imperialists who smashed cultures, desecrated ancestral graves, exploited land and labour and, at the same time, urged love of neighbour. So the self-accusation runs; and there is truth in it. We cannot but take with the utmost seriousness the challenge of a Hindu observer at the Nairobi Assembly of the World Council of Churches in 1975. Referring to the Christians there he said, "You would like all of us to come to be like you are, Christians. Thank you, I am not interested. Because, from you people, from the West, has come colonization, imperialism, pollution, the atomic war, etc."[13] The point was long ago taken by Forsyth: "When we have not persecuted, or neglected, the heathen we have exploited them. We have been careless what became of them provided we made fortunes out of them...We have introduced our curses and vices amongst them...vile liquor, horrible and shameful diseases, gunpowder, the slave-trade, blackbirding, treachery, and general contempt."[14] His judgment was that "it is one of the banes of our missionary enterprise that it comes to the heathen from a dominant militant race...Oh! why does our method not oftener preach our message?"[15] As a young man Forsyth was horrified by Bishop Ellicott's voting for the Afghan War because it might be the means of getting Christianity and the Bible into Afghanistan.[16]

But, as so often, there is a balance to be struck. First, the attitudes of the early missionary societies were by no means always imperialistic. Listen to the charter of the London Missionary Society (1797):

> As the union of Christians of various denominations in carrying on this great work is a most desirable object, so, to prevent, if possible, any cause of future dissension, it is declared to be a *fundamental principle of The Missionary Society* that its design is not to send Presbyterianism, Independency, Episcopacy, or any other form of Church Order and Government (about which there may be difference of opinion among serious persons), but the glorious Gospel of the blessed God, to the heathen; and that it shall be left (as it ought to be left) to the minds of the persons whom God may call into the fellowship of His Son from among them to assume for themselves such form of Church Government as to them shall appear most agreeable to the Word of God.[17]

You will observe that the intention of exporting a specific church order is here strenuously disavowed — which was just as well, because, for example, "the nature of Samoan village life made it almost impossible to give reality the separated church meeting in the Congregational sense."[18] Rather, the motive was to proclaim "the glorious Gospel of the blessed God," and to allow those who became Christians to work out their own church order in a manner "agreeable to the Word of God."

Now hear Lesslie Newbigin, one of this century's most distinguished missionary statesmen:

> On page after page of the history of Asia, Africa and the Pacific Islands, you will find missionaries laying the foundations for the cultural revivals of the twentieth century, reducing languages to writing, revitalizing stagnant languages, rediscovering the forgotten past of ancient cultures and creating a new pride in them, and protecting the living cultures from destruction. You will find them also in countless cases standing up, often alone, on behalf of peoples unable to stand up for themselves against the slave-trader and the blackbirder, the exploiting of cheap labour by industry, and the over-riding of native interests by colonial governments. These things must be taken into account if a balance sheet is to be drawn.[19]

The Dutch missologist, Johannes Verkuyl, while admitting that "there is much reason for [missionary] self-criticism" also observes that "the critics sometimes remind one of the flagellants of the middle ages, with the difference that the flagellants castigated themselves, but the modern flagellants usually castigate the missionaries of the past, while cherishing and patting themselves on the back for their insight."[20]

Despite all intellectual and other obstacles, there is renewal and church growth — sometimes rapid church growth — in many parts of the world. It is said that in 1925 there were twenty-five million Christians in Africa; today there are well over one hundred million Christians there; and by the end of this century it is expected that Africa will contain the largest concentration of Christians in the world — a prospect with which the traditionally strong Christian West has yet fully to come to terms. It has been estimated that in Europe and North America an average of 53,000 people leave the churches each week; in Africa 115,000 join the churches each week.[21] Elsewhere the story is different. In India, after two hundred years of toil by thousands of missionaries, Christians number less than three per cent of the total population. On which fact the Indian scholar K.M. Pannikar commented: "It will hardly be denied that, in spite of the immense and sustained effort made by the Churches with the support of the lay public of the European countries and America, the attempt to conquer Asia for Christ has definitely failed."[22] You will note that the reference in that quotation was to Asia, not just to India; and now, thirty-five years since those words were written some qualification is called for. During those years the Christian population of South Korea has risen to twenty-five per cent of the total population in that country; there is rapid growth in Indonesia and elsewhere; but still not in India. On all of which three points may be made. First, growth in numbers is not the most important thing; and where there is a shortage of leadership it can militate against growth in depth. Secondly, although Christians have traditionally believed that the Gospel is to be proclaimed to the ends of the earth, there is no New Testament warrant for supposing that God cannot bring his purposes to pass unless or until everyone in the world has been converted: there is too much concerning the faithful remnant in the Bible for us to believe that; there is too much in church history and in the present day to remind us that the Church has usually been at its most faithful when it has been at its most oppressed and confined. Thirdly, those whose faith includes a Good Friday ought to be wary of pronouncing failure too quickly. Indeed, as far as Asia is concerned, one scholar has suggested that

> without in any way disparaging the heroic efforts of missionaries in the past 200 years, it is possible to argue that the fully authentic Christian mission to Hindus and Buddhists has only just begun. It will be interesting to see what will happen as Asian Christian missionaries proclaim the gospel of Christ without the shadow of western military might in the background of their auditors' minds.[23]

This comment reminds us that it is now quite antiquated to think in terms of missionaries sent by the West and received by everybody else. Partnership in mission, which entails two-way traffic, is a concept which has come into its own during the past ten years, and which is increasingly being practised around the world; and this both on the theological ground that mission is the work of the Church in every place, and on the practical ground that the traditional sending countries now need themselves to receive missionaries from elsewhere, and that not only because of the expatriate communities in their midst. Christian mission of integrity is now to be seen as mission by, to and for the whole world.[24]

But at this point we have to note that Christianity is not the only world religion to be on the march. After a journey to the United States and Europe in the 1890s the Hindu Swami Vivekananda asked,

> Where are the men ready to go out to every country in the world with the message of the great sages of India? Where are the men who are ready to sacrifice everything so that this message shall reach every corner of this world? Such heroic souls are wanted to help spread the truth. Such heroic workers are wanted to go abroad and help; to disseminate the great truths of the Vedanta. The world wants it; without it the world will be destroyed.[25]

More recently a Muslim writer has explained that the people of his faith "are...charged with the noble mission of bringing the whole world to its Supreme Sovereign, and of freeing it from servitude to any false god. The propagation of Islam to all people is a religious duty which must be undertaken by all true Muslims..."[26]

When to the renewal and missionary zeal of some other faiths is added the fact of guilt which many Christians feel in respect of imperialism and exploitation, the question of the right to evangelize often comes to the fore. Thus, for example, George

Lindbeck has said that "the missionary task of Christians may at times be to encourage Marxists to become better Marxists, Jews and Muslims to become better Jews and Muslims, and Buddhists to become better Buddhists..."[27] I suspect that even these words sound presumptuous to some people of those persuasions; and I underline Dr. Lindbeck's qualification that what he suggests may *at times* be the appropriate policy. But clearly, if that policy were ever to become general, the question of the truth of the claims made by the several religions and ideologies would not and could not be raised. Some Christians might be content with such a state of affairs, but there is no guarantee that all members of other faiths would be; and probably most Christians would continue to feel that they are under the obligation of testifying to what they have seen and heard — and to its *truth.*

Having now indicated some of the pitfalls in this kind of enquiry, I had better now return to base, and then see if it is possible to move forward.

 II

Can Christians claim with integrity to have a mission to the whole world? Certainly they cannot base an affirmative answer to that question upon their own status or worth. In the deepest sense their motive to mission does not originate with them at all. Its origins are in God the Holy Trinity:

> We are the beneficiaries of eternity [wrote P.T. Forsyth]. The power that claims and saves us is from beyond history, from before the foundation of the world. The first missionary was God the Father, who sent forth His Son in the likeness of sinful flesh. That is the seal and final ground of missions — the grace...of God...who gave us not only a prophet but a propitiation. The second missionary was that Son, the apostle of our profession...who...humbled Himself to death, even death of the Cross. And the third missionary is the Holy Ghost, whom the Saviour sends forth into all the earth...And the fourth missionary is the Church. And these four missionaries are all involved in the one Divine redemption to which we owe ourselves utterly.[28]

Behind this trinitarian way of grounding mission are such Biblical passages as this from Jesus's High-Priestly prayer: "As thou hast sent me into the world, I have sent them [that is, the apostles] into the world."[29] In recent years an impressive ecumenical convergence on the ground of Christian mission has been developing. I select four examples from many. Hear first an Orthodox theologian:

> The eternally active mission of love in the Holy Trinity...could not remain in Heaven leaving fallen humanity to its destiny, but descended again to the world to redeem them through his passion, death, resurrection, and he again

descended into the Church at Pentecost to create an egalitarian sharing humanity of the redeemed children of God. The same agape that empties itself on the cross to create one family in the model of the triune Godhead is the distinguishing mark of Christian mission at all times.[30]

Next, a sentence from the National Conference of Catholic Bishops of the U.S.A.: "The missionary task of the church is rooted theologically in the Blessed Trinity. The very origin of the church is from the missions of the Son and the Holy Spirit as decreed by the Father...who desires the salvation of the whole human race."[31] Now an Anglican theologian:

> Mission does not begin with the Church: it originates in the redemptive purpose of the triune God. It is therefore not just an extension of the Church...it is only by recognizing that mission is *missio dei*...that there is any escape from the vicious circle that begins from the Church and ends with the Church, which is to turn ecclesiology into ecclesiolatry.[32]

Finally, a Reformed theologian, Samuel Volbeda: "God as the triune God qualifies as the subject or author of missions.[33]

If the Church takes all of this seriously it will realize the inescapability of mission. The Church does not choose whether to be missionary or not. To be the Church is to be involved in God's mission: it is to be sent by him. Moreover, the realization that mission originates in the divine Trinity should serve as the most powerful check possible upon missionary imperialism; for at the very least it means that the Gospel did not originate in West, East, North or South, but in eternity itself. I shall return to this point at the end of this lecture. For the moment we may say that the Church cannot with integrity refuse the call to mission.

At least, we may say this in principle; but in practice the nagging question persists, Why us? Here we are face to face with the so-called scandal of particularity. why did God become Incarnate here and not there? Why did he choose these people and not those to be the bearers of his Gospel in the world? At this point I have to be agnostic. I simply do not know why God should have acted as he did, and neither does anyone else. But some mitigating comments may be made. First, those who may wish to argue that we cannot deduce universal truths from historical particulars are ruling out the possibility of divine revelation from the start. Christians cannot do that because of what they have seen of God, and received from him, supremely in the Cross-Resurrection event. As for the charge of exclusivist unfairness, we must remember that the Biblical doctrine of election never suggests that the divine choice falls on individuals or groups because of their intrinsic worth. Israel was reminded of this in no uncertain terms: "It was not because you were more numerous than any other nation that the Lord cared for you and chose you, for you were the smallest of all nations."[34] Moreover, the call is not to be God's favourites, but to be his agents; and there is no privilege without responsibility. From those to whom much has been given, much will be expected. This is the consistent teaching of the prophets of old and of Jesus himself.[35] The calling of the church is to unstinting service after the pattern of the One who, though Lord, washed his disciples' feet, and gave himself for all.

The ultimate justification of Christian mission, then, is that God gives life and salvation in the Christ he sent, and that Christ in turn sends out those who receive that gift to bear witness to it. It is important that we begin from this realization; otherwise the danger will be that we shall try to justify mission on purely utilitarian grounds. That is, we may be tempted to say that the reason for Christian mission is that education, health care, irrigation projects and other development programmes are launched under the initiative of Christian missions. So they are — and a good thing too, for Christian mission of integrity has to do with the whole person and the whole environment — and this in response to the teaching and example of Jesus, who healed the sick, fed the hungry and challenged his followers to a holistic mission. But if we think only in utilitarian terms we have to ask, "What do we that right-minded humanists do not?" If ever we are tempted to think that social service is the justification of mission, we need to remember that

> The Church is first a priest to God and then a blessing to men. The popular idea of the Church...is quite wrong. It regards it as an instrument for social service, with no more sacrifice, worship, or thought than contributes to that end. This is an idea of the Church which is inevitable wherever faith has ceased to find its object in the atonement Christ made to God, and is transferred to the pity Christ spent on men.[36]

In passing, I should like to suggest that we are not utilitarian enough where the needs of the doubting, apathetic or agnostic intellectual are concerned. Writing from his Canadian university perspective, Joseph McLelland declares that

> We [that is, Christians] have become irrelevant to those who will run the world in the future, who will make choices about war and peace, life and death...A professor of philosophy thinks every Christian must be a 'naive supernaturalist'; a chemistry professor asks what possible benefit 'Presbyterian dogma' could be to the search for knowledge; biology students seek help in trying to relate their conservative theology...with evolution; psychology and sociology, even medicine and law and education, assume that human beings can be explained without reference to God...That's what bothers me in my daily mission field of the modern university.[37]

In a word, we need a new apologetic; and our entirely proper concern for the poor and disadvantaged should not allow us to forget that few things did more, humanly speaking, to propagate the Christian faith in the intellectually diverse world of the early centuries than the fact that the Gospel captured some of the ablest minds of the day.

To return from this digression: the understanding of the trinitarian basis of Christian mission also challenges the whole Church as to its ecumenical task. The ecumenical vision is that the "whole inhabited earth" shall come to unity in Christ. The Church is called to be a foretaste of God's final reconciliation of all things. But, as we well know, the empirical Church is rent asunder. Called and sent by God, the first missionary, we are not even reconciled to one another at the Lord's table. This cannot but weaken the message of reconciliation which we proclaim. This is why it is so sad when Christians say, I am for mission, or I am for ecumenism, or I am for social service — as if these were mutually exclusive alternatives. On the contrary, they are inextricably interwoven; the neglect of any one of them reduces our proclamation to a sham; and we shall not begin to achieve integrity in mission unless we realize that this is so, and act accordingly.[38] The Gospel which reconciles us to God unites us to all his people, and commissions us to service.

III

What, no doubt, is now becoming clear, is that serious thought on the question of mission involves serious thought on every Christian doctrine. Already the idea of mission has prompted us to think about the Trinity, the Church, and humanity in its need of redemption and of human well-being. I now wish to point out that thought about mission cannot but prompt reflection upon the doctrine of creation. And here we return once again to that most persistent of contemporary missiological questions, How are we to behave in relation to the non-Christian majority in the world? We need integrity in the sense of honesty when considering those of other cultures and faiths who, with us, share a threatened and a divided world. I shall suggest that since Christians are called to bear witness to Christ in all circumstances of life, they cannot properly desist from this task where those of other faiths, or of non-faith, are concerned. But their witness must be characterized by integrity in relation to the Gospel and to those to whom they witness.

What does this mean? Integrity in relation to the Gospel has to do with what is said, and with the manner in which it is said; indeed, it has to do with the whole bearing of the Christian towards the other. The Gospel should determine the manner. For the Good News of God's love is a gracious word, and its propagation will not be assisted by gracelessness. Moreover, it is a world for the whole world, but it is the word of One who is present before we go, and whether we go or not. This is where the doctrine of creation comes in. If, as Christians believe, God is the creator of all; if humans are made in his image so that there is, as the Quakers say, "that of God in every man," then none are excluded from his loving care, and God cannot be excluded from any part of his creation. As the psalmist sang, God's "tender care rests upon all his creatures."[39] Though transcendent over all things, he is immanent within all things, for he made them all.

But all is not well. Though all are God's children, not all are sons by the adoption of grace, as Paul would say. Knowing the truth, humans stifle it.[40] The divine image is defaced, though not obliterated — otherwise we should no longer be responsible beings. What God has done to restore us is at the heart of the Christian's witness.[41] In making this witness Christians must avoid a number of pitfalls.

First, we must not suppose that *we* could convert anyone. God is sovereign in salvation; he alone can take the scales from people's eyes; by his Spirit alone does the work of regeneration — new birth — begin. Like Peter and John, Christians are constrained by what they have seen and heard;[42] but while they may be responsible for any amount of missionary bungling, they are not responsible for anyone's conversion. No one is more abominable than the aggressive evangelist who piles psychological pressure upon psychological pressure so that, in commercial style, he can submit good returns to his financial masters. Such an approach lacks integrity both in relation to the Gospel and in relation to the other people. As to the Gospel, it does not permit God to be the Saviour; as to the hearers (or victims!), it denigrates God's free children by regarding them as objects to be manipulated rather than as people to be loved.

Unjustifiable pressure can also be exerted in material ways, especially in economically disadvantaged and desperately needy areas of the world. True, I have never seen a placard outside a mission hospital inscribed, "Lose your tonsils and find a Saviour," but the temptation to try to bribe people in the Kingdom (or to entice them away from other parts of Christ's fold) is sometimes strong; and there is sometimes a very thin line indeed between that, and the proper desire to make the most of opportunities for witness which practical service of all kinds provides.

Secondly, we must have due regard to the context in which we are witnessing. Pedagogically, and in terms of evangelism, this means that we must seek to relate our message to the experience of those among whom we go. The point is so obvious that I shall not labour it here.[43] It will suffice if I caution you to remember the narrow-minded Christian Englishman who went to preach in the Republic of Ireland. In the course of his sermon he denounced women who paint their lips the colour of mail boxes. Thereupon, to his great surprise, unrestrained mirth broke out. He had forgotten that in Ireland, mail boxes are painted green, not red. More important for our present purpose is the *moral* importance of the context. Are we in a context of evangelism; or education; or dialogue with those of other faiths? We need to be clear on this if we are to proceed with integrity. A classroom is not a mission hall. A dialogue is not the occasion for evangelizing.

Just as, in the public classroom, the teacher of Religious Studies is overstepping the mark if he or she regards the classroom as a mission field, so in dialogue with people of other faiths the objective is mutual sharing and growth in knowledge and respect. We are not there to browbeat the other, but to learn from one another. At the same time, there will be no integrity in the dialogue unless all parties feel free to bear witness to their most cherished convictions — something which, if they are wise, and having regard to the besmirched records of all the religions, they will do with becoming humility. On many practical issues of the day, and on the basis of an acceptance of at least a weak form of natural law theory,[44] they may find a common platform for testimony and service in the field of human rights, peace, and the like. But doctrine is the crucial area, and I think that here four moves are ruled out.

First, we cannot with integrity abstract doctrines from the total world view of which they form a part in the hope of securing doctrinal agreement with those of another faith. Thus, even if it could be shown that all religions uphold a doctrine of creation, this would be but a minimal claim. The General Secretary of the World Council of Churches has put the point clearly:

> It is impossible for Christians now to go back to the story of the creation and to read it as if Jesus Christ had not come. We cannot discuss the being of humankind without the self-disclosure of humanity in the same Jesus of Nazareth. And, obviously, all our image perceptions of the God to whom we pray are dependent on the image of God that we have perceived in Jesus Christ. It would therefore be cheating our friends of other religions if we pretended to be neutral in our approaches to subjects such as nature, humankind, or God, when they are very much, in fact, related to the life, ministry, death and resurrection of Jesus Christ.[45]

After all, Christians believe that the God of creation so identities himself with his creatures as to become incarnate in Jesus, and there's the rub once more. And the heart of the Christian doctrine of creation is not to be found in Genesis, but in John: "The word, then, was with God from the beginning, and through him all things came to be."[46]

Secondly, we cannot, motivated by the desire to be genial and inoffensive, proceed as if the question of truth does not arise. It is sometimes said that all religions display aspects of the truth. They are spokes of a wheel, or facets of a diamond. Now clearly, the truth is the truth wherever it is found. But the spokes-of-a-wheel approach cannot with integrity be used to paper over differences between contradictory religious claims. Of some pairs of such claims — where one claim emanates from one religion, the other from another — we have simply to say that one or the other may be true, or both may be false, but they cannot both be true. The same would seem to apply to a single claim such as "Christ is the Saviour of the world." If Christians wish to make that assertion, and if those of another faith, or of no faith, wish to assert, "It is not the case that Christ is the Saviour of the world," then I cannot see that relativism can get a look-in here. All are wishing to say more than that "What I say is true for me, but not perhaps for you; today, but not perhaps tomorrow." Moreover, were Christians to seek to promote concord via relativism, they would be tacitly denying the propriety of others in making claims which they wish to be regarded as absolute.

The Christian must not be offensive; but no Christian can remove the offence of the Cross. It is scandalous in the sense of being a stumbling-block. The Christian faith does make the claim that at the Cross-Resurrection event God acted once and for all for the salvation of the world. We do not display integrity in the Gospel if we deny this; we do not display integrity with our dialogue partner if we bracket this claim. But the exclusivity of Christianity "is not a sectional exclusiveness. [Christ] is not the exclusive possession of a sect; he is the exclusive possession of all mankind."[47] For this reason, and also because of the doctrines of creation and grace, those evangelicals who declared at Chicago in 1960 that "in the years since the war, more than one billion souls have passed into eternity and more than half of these went to the torment of hellfire without even hearing of Jesus Christ,"[48] were offensive in the bad and unnecessary sense. How can these Christians be so sure of the eternal destination of anyone, since they are not God, and since the New Testament gives plenty of scope for the thought that the "religious" will have a number of surprises when they discover who their eternal companions are, and are not?[49] Such pre-critical exclusiveness completely undermines the inclusiveness of the Gospel of the grace of God.

Thirdly, we must take care how we apply the idea of God's transcendence. We saw in an earlier lecture[50] that a declared motive on the part of the authors of *The Myth of God Incarnate* (1977) was that of facing up to contemporary religious pluralism, with special reference to Christian relations with those of other faiths. There can be little doubt that this is an urgent necessity; the task must be undertaken with integrity both in respect of the Gospel and towards people of other faiths. As the old cartographers said, "Here be dragons!" As far as the Christian Gospel is concerned, we have not done justice to it unless we declare that in the Cross-Resurrection event God acted once and for all for the redemption of the world. If we sit loose to the doctrine of Atonement we shall be the more easily content with a reduced Christology. The Incarnation can then become a myth which symbolizes the timeless truth that God comes to be near humanity — not least in our suffering. John Hick has succinctly expressed his view thus:

> I would put it that salvation (or the creation of children of God) is the work of God-in-relation-to man, and that the christian name for this universal saving power is the Logos, or Spirit, or Christ, or Second Person of the Trinity. But there are also non-christian names for this universal saving power, which or who has operated in varying ways and degrees both in Jesus of Nazareth and also in other human beings and other religious movements. It is thus true (but a truth expressed in the language of one particular tradition) that all salvation is through the Christ or the universal Logos; but it is not true that all salvation is through Jesus of Nazareth.[51]

Here we see clearly that the emphasis is upon a universal Logos, not upon a specific, once-for-all redemptive act in history. But if, as I wish to maintain, Christianity as traditionally understood has been centrally concerned with precisely such an act, then the question arises whether what Dr. Hick is seeking to relate to other faiths would be recognized as Christianity by most Christians living or dead. It is logically possible that the bulk of Christians in every age has been misguided in its convictions; but we should not be treating those of other faiths with integrity if we misled them into thinking that Dr. Hick's revisionist Christianity were fully representative of the Christian faith as generally received. It need hardly be said that Dr. Hick is perfectly well aware that his stance will be repudiated by those whom he calls "conservative believers"; and it must be said that some have reacted against Dr. Hick with a singular lack of grace. But conservative, though a slippery term, [52] need not be taken in a pejorative sense. It can be used to designate those who, with good reason, feel that there is more in the Gospel to be conserved from age to age than Dr. Hick allows.

Dr. Hick seeks to persuade those of other faiths that all of us are in fact making a response to one transcendent divine reality, which Christians call the Logos, but to which others give other names. [53] Now this may not at all be what some of other faiths think they are doing, and we only throw an offensive obstacle in the path of dialogue if we suppose otherwise. Moreover, this is a move which can be made only by ignoring some of the fundamental and conflicting truth claims of the several religions, including the Christian. As Duncan Forrester has written, "Hick believes, it appears, that all religions in their, 'experiential roots' are in contact with the same ultimate reality, but that only the differences in the understanding of that reality are culturally determined 'secondary, human, historical developments.' One wonders whether perhaps he has not capitulated to a relativism which is unlikely to be acceptable to committed believers except for Vedantic Hindus." [54] Indeed, some have gone so far as to suggest that in his own way, and despite his avowed intention, Dr. Hick is more than a little imperialistic in supposing that *he* has located that absolute towards which all the religions are tending, or to which they are all imperfectly witnessing. [55] We can at least understand why some consider that Dr. Hick is in the line of idealists of every age (and of the New Age [56]) to whom the stuff of history is, in the last resort, of little consequence. Where understandings of the divine transcendence are not balanced by notions of a God acting immanently in history and on history's stage, the Gospel is at risk.

Fourthly, we must beware of making our testimony in such a way as to suggest that those of other faiths, and of no faith, are, if only they would realize it, crypto-Christians or anonymous Christians. This move has a long history. A number of the early Fathers thought of some of the Greek philosophers as being Christians before Christ. Thus, for example, Justin Martyr declares that "those who lived reasonably are Christians, even though they have been thought atheists; as, among the Greeks, Socrates and Heraclitus, and men like them; and among the barbarians, Abraham...and many others..." [57] Again, in the Reformation period we find Zwingli making generous remarks about those whom he calls the "pious heathen." "There has not been a good man," he declares, "and will not be a holy heart or faithful soul from the beginning of the world to the end thereof that you will not see in heaven with God." [58] The objective of recognizing the good wherever it is found is laudable, but if morals are autonomous, as I have claimed that they are in an earlier lecture,[59] we do not need to label all of the good Christian. Indeed, we will rightly offend some if we do; we will appear to coerce, or to patronize, and to take their own actual profession with less than due seriousness. The way of imperialistic annexation sits ill with the way of dialogue. The motives which lead some to overlook this fact are varied. In referring to "anonymous Christians" the Roman Catholic theologian Karl Rahner was seeking to modify the teaching of the Council of Florence (1438–45) to the effect that those who die outside of the Catholic Church "go to the everlasting fire prepared for the devil and his angels."[60] A motive surely to be applauded! Again, when the Presbyterian theologian John Baillie spoke of those who believe in the bottom of their hearts while denying with the top of their heads,[61] he had the humanists and agnostics of the present-day West primarily in mind. But Professor H.D. Lewis rightly pointed out that Baillie's stance permits the believer's opponent to return the charge of self-deception, and that the evidence that, for example, Bertrand Russell was a secret believer is notoriously difficult to find.[62] Furthermore, how can we with integrity deny the right and ability of others to express *their* deepest convictions with integrity? To deny that all are believers at heart is not to deny the Christian doctrine of our creation in the divine image — that is, our creation as constitutionally capable of relations with God, and as actually manifesting something of him no matter what we believe. It is simply to allow others to speak the truth as they see it.

The General Secretary of the World Council of Churches may sum the matter up for us. He refers to people of other faiths, but what he says applies also to Marxists and to those of no religion or ideology at all. With reference to the "anonymous Christians" line of approach he writes,

> The positive side of this is the recognition of the values and virtues of many people within the most diverse religious systems that illustrate the kind of Christian values that we would like to see defended, expanded, assured and confirmed everywhere. We cannot avoid having the impression that behind this 'baptism' of others we are applying a sort of spiritual paternalism, a certain moral superiority that we presuppose in the Christian community that will accredit others are Christians. Our fellow human being wants to be recognized by his or her own identity with the particular community to which he or she belongs. Only in that way can we avoid condescending attitudes and fully respect our partner; then the give and take of a witnessing encounter can take place.[63]

IV

It is time to draw these reflections to a close. I have suggested that mission is integral to the work of the Triune god, who sent his Son who, in turn, sends the Spirit and the Church. The Church comprises those who are sent forth in the name of the

God of all grace, who is judge and Lord of all. The implications of the doctrines of humanity and of creation concerning the manner in which we go must be heeded; and we must continue to go and bear witness until God's consummation of all things.

The mention of God's consummation brings me to my final point. The work is God's and he is patient. We are called to be industrious and obedient, not frantic. The mission is in the hands of the Lord of history. This is another way of saying that we cannot eradicate the supernatural. God the Lord has acted in creation and redemption, and these actions are the controlling features of the Christian understanding of history. Some say that we should emphasize the Kingdom — that is, the kingly reign — of God, because Jesus made so much of it in his own teaching. No doubt the idea of God's eternal reign is fundamental to the Christian understanding of history. But in preaching the Cross, Christians have intended to highlight the paradigm case of the triumph of that Kingdom over sin, over all that could keep humanity from God. As P.T. Forsyth wrote,

> The Cross was not central to Christ's teaching as the kingdom was; but it was central to what is more than his teaching — to His healing, to His Person, work, and victory. It is more original than His teaching, and more universal...Christianity spread, not as a religion of truth, but of power, help, healing, resurrection, redemption.[64]

This affirmation should, perhaps, be qualified by the comment that Christianity does claim to be a religion of truth; Forsyth means that it is not simply one more collection of teachings.

But while Christians assert the certainty of God's final victory because the crucial battle has been fought and won at the Cross, they have, to return to my earlier point, no assurance that the conversion of the whole world to Christ is the necessary and inevitable prelude to the consummation. The mission is that of the triune God who sent his Son; and he met with misunderstanding, hostility, rejection, death. There is no reason for the Church to expect that its reception and fate will be any different from that of its Lord. The blood of countless missionary martyrs testifies to this. But Christians still take up their cross, and do so with hope and courage because of the victory won. As R.K. Orchard wrote, "God's reign is over all, and is not dependent on human testimony to it."[65] Nor, I would add, is it dependent upon human acknowledgement of it.

"What matters," wrote Lesslie Newbigin of Christians, "is that we would know Him, know that there is none to be feared beside Him, none to be loved except Him, nothing to be desired beside Him; know both the fellowship of His sufferings and the power of His resurrection, both His power and His peace, so that we may be the bearers of His peace to all the nations."[66]

All the rest we can safely leave with the triune God, whose mission it is, and whose gracious purposes cannot fail.

NOTES

1. "American Congregational theology," A commission report presented at the fourth International Congregational Council. See *Proceedings*, 1920, 255.

2. Acts 10: 1–11: 18.

3. Adrian Saravia, *A treatise on the different degrees of the Christian Priesthood* (Latin original, London 1590; reprint, 1840) 180. For this and the two preceding points I am indebted to James Tanis, "Reformed Pietism and Christian Mission, *Harvard Theological Review* LXCVII (1, January 1974): 65–73. Mr. Tanis cites Beza's *Ad tractationem De ministrorum evangelii gradibus, ab Hadriano Saravia Belga editam, Theodori Bezae responsio*, (Geneva 1592), 113, and R. Pierce Beaver, "The Genevan Mission to Brazil," *The Reformed Journal* XVII (6, 1967): 14–20.

4. John Ryland Jr. seriously questioned this story concerning his father. See his *The Work of Faith, the Labour of Love, and the Patience of Hope Illustrated in the Life and Death of the Reverend Andrew Fuller* (London: Button & Son, 1816), 175. Nevertheless the tale is told by A.C. Underwood, *A History of the English Baptists* (London: Kingsgate Press, 1947), 142.

5. For a detailed account of the theology underlying the reluctance of some to engage in mission see Alan P.F. Sell, *The Great Debate: Calvinism, Arminianism and Salvation* (Worthing: H.E. Walter, 1982; now distributed by Word Books of Bletchley; Grand Rapids: Baker Book House, 1983).

6. Jonathan Edwards, *Works* (1834; reprint, Edinburgh: The Banner of Truth Trust, 1974), II:10.

7. Luke 19: 1–10. See further Lecture II above.

8. P.T. Forsyth, *Missions in State and Church* (London: Hodder & Stoughton, 1908), 16.

9. I Cor. 9:16.

10. T.F. Torrance, "Concerning Amsterdam," *Scottish Journal of Theology* II (3, 1949): 268.

11. See further, N.F.S. Ferré, *The Atonement and Mission* (London: London Missionary Society, 1960).

12. P.T. Forsyth, *Missions*, 19.

13. *Your Kingdom Come. Mission Perspectives. Report on the World Conference on Mission and Evangelism, Melbourne...1980* (Geneva: World Council of Churches, 1980), 33.

14. P.T. Forsyth, *Missions*, 265.

15. Ibid., 22.

16. Ibid, 117.

17. Norman Goodall, *A History of the London Missionary Society 1895–1945* (London: Oxford University Press, 1954), 3.

18. Ibid., 367.

19. Lesslie Newbigin, *A Faith for this One World?* (London: SCM Press, 1961), 107–8. See also Stephen Neill, *Colonialism and Christian Missions* (New York: McGraw-Hill, 1966); Arthur Schlesinger Jr., "The Missionary Enterprise and Imperialism," in *The Missionary Enterprise in China and America*, ed. John K. Fairbank (Cambridge, Mass.: Harvard University Press, 1974). In relation to missionary iconoclasm Allen Birtwhistle wrote, "it was more often Africans themselves, knowing the potency of these things [i.e. 'idols'], who were more ruthless than the missionaries." See his *They Who Will Hear* (London: Epworth, 1961), 117n.

20. J. Verkuyl, "The Unfinished Task of World Mission," *Occasional Essays of Latin American Center for Pastoral Studies*, San Jose, Costa Rica, VI (1–2, December 1979): 44–45.

21. See David J. Bosch, "Vision for mission," *International Review of Mission* XXVI, (301, January 1987): 13.

22. K.M. Pannikar, *Asia and Western Dominance* (London: Allen & Unwin, 1953), 454.

23. Dewi Arwel Hughes, "Christianity and Other Religions: A Review of Some Recent Discussion," *Themelios* IX (2, January 1984): 16.

24. For adjustments to the new situation see e.g., *The Ad Hoc Report on World Mission* (New York: Reformed Church in America, 1980).

25. *The Complete Works of Vivekananda*, 1924–32, III:276; quoted in *My Neighbour's Faith and Mine* (Geneva: World Council of Churches, 1986), 29.

26. Badru D. Kateregga and David W. Shenk, *Islam and Christianity: A Muslim and a Christian in Dialogue* (Grand Rapids: Eerdmans, 1981), 76.

27. G. Lindbeck, *The Nature of Doctrine* (Philadelphia: Westminster Press, 1984), 54.

28. P.T. Forsyth, *Missions*, 270.

29. John 17: 18.

30. Geevarghese Mar Osthathios, "The Gospel of the Kingdom and the Crucified and Risen Lord," in *Your Kingdom Come*, 42.

31. *To the Ends of the Earth. A Pastoral Statement on World Mission*, quoted in *International Bulletin of Missionary Research* XI (2, April 1987): 52.

32. J.G. Davies, *Worship and Mission* (London: SCM Press, 1966), 49.

33. Quoted by R. Recker, "The concept of the *Missio Dei* and Instruction in Mission at Calvin Seminary, *Calvin Theological Journal* XI (2, November 1976): 193.

34. Deuteronomy 7: 7.

35. Cf. e.g. Amos 3: 2; Matthew 25: 31– 46.

36. P.T. Forsyth, *Missions*, 21.

37. Joseph C. McLelland, "What does 'Jesus is Lord' mean Today?" *Presbyterian Record* (Canada), June 1988, 16.

38. Welcome emphasis is laid upon this point in the report of the Anglican-Reformed International Commission. See *God's Reign and Our Unity* (London: SPCK and Edinburgh: The Saint Andrew Press, 1984), 20–22.

39. Psalm 145: 9.

40. Romans 1: 18.

41. See further Lecture II above.

42. Acts 4: 20.

43. See Lecture I above for further reference to the context of proclamation.

44. See further Lecture III above.

45. Emilio Castro, "Mission in a Pluralistic Age," *International Review of Mission* LXXV (299, July 1986): 204–5.

46. John 1: 2,3; Cf. Colossians 1: 16.

47. P.T. Forsyth, *Missions*, 208. Cf. E. Castro, *Your Kingdom Come*, 35; also W.A. Visser't Hooft, *No Other Name* (London: SCM Press, 1963).

48. *Facing the Unfinished Task* (Grand Rapids: Eerdmans, 1961), 9.

49. See e.g. Matthew 25: 31–46.

50. See Lecture II above.

51. In a personal letter to John Ferguson, quoted by permission in *Reform*, February 1975, 11.

52. See Alan P.F. Sell, *Theology in Turmoil: The Roots, Course and Significance of the Conservative - Liberal Debate in Modern Theology* (Grand Rapids: Baker Book House, 1986), Ch. V.

53. See further John Hick, *Problems of Religious Pluralism* (New York: St. Martin's Press, 1985).

54. D.B. Forrester in *Scottish Journal of Theology* XXIX: 69.

55. See e.g. L. Newbigin, *The Open Secret* (London: SPCK, 1978), 185. D.A. Hughes, art.cit., 18. For a fuller statement and defence of his position see J. Hick, *An Interpretation of Religion: Human Responses to the Transcendent* (London: Macmillan, 1989).

56. Thus John W. Cooper defines the New Age Movement as an "evolutionary spiritual monism." See his "Testing the Spirit of the New Age of Aquarius: The New Age Movement," *Calvin Theological Journal* XXII (2, November, 1987): 297.

57. Justin Martyr, *I Apol.* XLVI. See further Alan P.F. Sell, "Theology and the Philosophical Environment: Some Case Studies from the Second Century A.D.," *Vox Evangelica* XIII (1983): 41–66 and XIV (1984): 53–64. Cf. William Penn: "The humble, meek, merciful, just, pious and devout souls are everywhere of one religion, and when death has taken off the mask they will know one another, although the diverse liveries they wear here make them strangers." From his *Reflections and Maxims*, quoted by Dan Seeger, *The Place of Universalism in the Society of Friends* (Leicester: Quaker Universalist Group, 1986), 12.

58. *The Latin Works of Huldreich Zwingli*, ed. Samuel M. Jackson (New York: Knickerbocker Press, 1912), II: 272; quoted by Timothy George, *Theology of the Reformers*, (Nashville: Broadman Press, 1988), 124.

59. See lecture III above.

60. See e.g. K. Rahner, *Theological Investigations* (Baltimore: Helicon, 1969), Ch. VI.

61. See e.g. J. Baillie, *The Sense of the Presence of God* (London: Oxford University Press, 1962, 76–87.

62. H.D. Lewis, *Philosophy of Religion* (London: English Universities Press, 1965), 119–120.

63. E. Castro, "Mission in a Pluralistic Age," op.cit., 201–202.

64. P.T. Forsyth, *Missions*, 11.

65. R.K. Orchard, *Missions in a Time of Testing* (London: Lutterworth, 1964), 73.

66. L. Newbigin, *Is Christ Divided? A Plea for Christian Unity in a Revolutionary Age* (Grand Rapids: Eerdmans, 1961), 41.

PASTORAL INTEGRITY

PASTORAL INTEGRITY

The Archdeacon Cecil Swanson Lecture

In one important sense of the term, pastoral integrity means dealing honestly with people in pastoral relationships. This is by means always an easy task in a world in which issues are often less than clear-cut. Consider the so-called pastoral lie. "Pastor," says the terminally ill person, "Do you think I shall recover?" How is the pastor to reply? The questioner expects a direct answer; if it is a blunt "No," all hope may fade; if it is an equally blunt "Yes," honesty has not been served, though the patient's spirits may have been raised. Most ministers would, no doubt, avoid giving a direct yes or no answer to such a question, and would attempt to prepare the person for either eventuality. In the somewhat distant philosophical terms of Sir David Ross, the pastor has been confronted by a clash of prima facie duties. He has the duty to be honest; he has the duty to preserve the patient's will to live. This is but one of many ways in which pastoral situations can challenge our integrity, our honesty.

Sadly, it is not difficult to find examples from church history of failures in pastoral integrity. In this connection the tormented George Fox, the founder of the Society of Friends, comes to mind. He felt that he had been a dreadful sinner (though most us would regard visiting a fairground with other youths as, at worst, a youthful peccadillo); but Fox was in agony of soul for some time. He left home and roamed the countryside seeking solace. One day he called on an "ancient priest" — his way of describing an elderly clergyman of the Church of England — at Mancetter, Warwickshire. In his *Journal* Fox writes:

> I...reasoned with him about the ground of despair and temptations, but he was ignorant of my condition; and he bid me take tobacco and sing psalms.

> Tobacco was a thing I did not love and psalms I was not in an estate to
> sing...And he told my troubles and sorrows and griefs to his servants, so that
> it got among the milklasses, which grieved me that I should open my mouth
> to such a one. I saw they were all miserable comforters; and this brought my
> troubles more upon me.[1]

By any standards, this incident displays an utter lack of pastoral integrity. Fox was not
honestly dealt with, and his confidence was betrayed. Happily, as we know, he
eventually found the resolution of his troubles in Christ.

Important though pastoral honesty is, I do not wish to dwell upon honest and
dishonest responses in specific pastoral cases. Rather, I wish to focus upon integrity
in the sense of wholeness, and to suggest that the whole church — pastor, and people
alike — is challenged to be a whole people, ministered to by a whole pastor, making
a whole witness. The whole church is a pastoral unit or corps; the whole church
proclaims something by its life, attitudes, activities and structures. The church as a
whole is to be a community of praise, witness, mission and caring. Just as a minister
who proclaimed the love of God and then lived as if he had never heard of it would
rightly be branded a hypocrite — a play-actor — so a church which does the same
thing is denying and dishonouring its Lord.

Christians believe that they have a whole Gospel, some good news which goes to
the root of the human malaise and rebellion against God, and deals with it. They claim
that by God's grace — his overflowing love towards the undeserving — he has called
them to himself, and given them to one another in love and service. Is this how it
appears to those around? Some among those who in days of yore were called "the
worldlings" are remarkably adept at detecting the slightest difference between what
the Church claims to be proclaiming, and what it is actually proclaiming. No doubt
"the worldings" need to be reminded (as do some church members) that the Church
comprises sinners; it is an earthen vessel; and those who hanker after a supposed golden
age of the Church which they would be glad to recover have never carefully read the
New Testament, much of which would not have been written had Christians not been
misbehaving in one way or another. In Thessalonica the mission of the church was
going by the board while many of the Christians were lazily awaiting the End; in
Corinth the Lord's Supper had been turned into a drunken orgy; and in Galatia the
Gospel was being distorted by addition. The fact remains, however, that if, as Paul
insisted, we are saved by grace and not by works, there is, as the letter of James makes
plain, no real faith which does not issue in good works. The redeemed community is
challenged to be a redemptive society; and a redemptive society is a society of integrity,
of wholeness. Those who have been made whole by grace are called to model that
unity in society as an earnest and sign of God's Kingdom.

Of the early Christians — and despite their failings — it was said in admiration,
not sarcasm, "See how these Christians love one another."[2] Their relationships were

characterized by mutual caring; they knew that they were challenged to love as they had been loved; and with God's help, sometimes at least they succeeded. Their pastoral care bore out the message they proclaimed. They were integrated wholes.

What, in more detail, makes for the wholeness, the integrity, of a local church? I shall suggest that such a church is one in fellowship, one in discipline and one in worship.

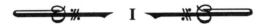

First, a church of integrity will be united in true Christian fellowship. This word fellowship is often used in ordinary life to characterize that spirit of friendship and union which binds those who share common interests. Fellowship can be found in male voice choirs, in sports, in amateur dramatics, and in many other spheres. Enthusiasts band together, organize themselves, and promote their interest. All of this fellowship, good as it is, is fellowship of the "horizontal" kind. By contrast, Christian fellowship is first a "vertical" matter. It does not come about because enthusiasts for a common interest organize themselves. It is a matter of the call of God. God takes the initiative; he engrafts us into Christ as branches are engrafted into the vine, and in that way people who share no interests of the ordinary kind find that they are united to one another, whether they like it or not.[3]

The metaphor of the vine and the branches is but one of a number of ways in which the New Testament speaks of the Church. The idea of the Church as the body of Christ is there too: a body having many limbs, or members, each with its own part to play in the working of the whole, and none able to say that it has no need of the others.[4] But the metaphor upon which I wish to dwell is that which described the Church as a royal and holy priesthood of believers.[5] What does this mean? We have already admitted that churches are not composed of paragons of virtue, so holy must mean something other than that. The idea is that holy people are those who are separated out and called together for a special purpose, for God's special use. By the time of the Christian era this was already an ancient notion: in the Old Testament, Israel is called to be "a kingdom of priests, my holy nation."[6]

Those so-called, whether in Israel or the Church, are *not* God's favourites, though sometimes they have thought that they were. They are in fact called to be God's agents and, precisely because of this special calling, they will be judged more severely than others if they fail. The prophet Amos came before God's people and thundered, "You only have I known of all the families of the earth, therefore I will punish you for your iniquities."[7] And Jesus himself reserved some of his sternest words for those who called him "Lord, Lord" — and then took no notice whatever of what he demanded of them.[8] The moral is that from those to whom much has been given, much will be expected.

Partly, no doubt, because of the encroachments of Enlightenment individualism, the corporate images of the Church, and especially the idea of the priesthood of all believers, have lost their real significance. In some Protestant circles it came to be understood that Luther had intended the doctrine to mean only that every person is a priest before God in the sense that, without the mediation of an ordained priest, every person could have direct access to God. Luther certainly did mean that. He interpreted I Peter 2: 9 as meaning that "Christ has so operated on us that we are able spiritually to act and pray on behalf of one another, just as the priest acts and prays bodily on behalf of the people."[9] In his three Tractates of 1520, and in his *de Instituendis Ministris* (1523) he further expounded the idea. But the context is always that of the fellowship, the community. He has in mind a company of priests whose status is conferred by their incorporation in Christ, the great High Priest. Luther is no individualist. Neither is Calvin, and in his Catechism of 1541, Calvin answers the question on the purpose of Christ's priestly office thus:

> First, by means of it He is the Mediator who reconciles us to God His Father; and secondly, through Him we have access to present ourselves to God, and offer Him ourselves in sacrifice with all that belongs to us. And in this way we are companions of His Priesthood.[10]

If the distinguished older historian of the Reformation, T.M. Lindsay, was right in saying that the doctrine of the priesthood of all believers "was the rock on which all attempts at reunion with an unreformed Christendom were wrecked,"[11] (and, because of the way in which the views of Luther and Calvin were pitted against Rome's concept and practice of the ordained priesthood, there is something in what he says), we can only take it as a hopeful sign that since Vatican II a considerable amount of fresh thinking has taken place in the Roman Catholic Church on this subject. The Roman Catholic writer, Peter Drilling, explains the more recent thought thus: "Within the Church of God both the priesthood common to all the Christian faithful and the ministerial priesthood are participations in the high priesthood of Christ, ways of being within the time and space of the historical Church of Jesus Christ that enable the whole People of God, and ultimately all those human beings who have come forth from God's creative hand, to be reconciled with God and find their home within the trinitarian divine community."[12]

These words could well have been written by my Presbyterian teacher, T.W. Manson, who did, in fact, declare that "the priesthood of all believers lies in the fact that each believer offers himself as a sacrifice according to the pattern laid down by Christ; and — what is equally essential — that all these individual offerings are taken up into the one perpetual offering made by the one eternal high-priest of the New Covenant."[13] Peter Drilling calls the "recovery of the doctrine of the church as the People of God and of the priestly character of all the People of God" momentous;[14] and so it is.

But despite the biblical warrant and the growing ecumenical convergence on the importance of the whole people of God as a fellowship, rampant individualism can still fragment the body. The priesthood of all believers can come to mean that everyone can do his or her own thing in the church; we all behave like unrelated atoms. At worst we have the situation portrayed so often in the book of Judges: "everyone did what was right in his own eyes." That way lies anarchy. So to my second point.

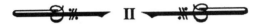

The members of a church of integrity will be a disciplined body. Undoubtedly, discipline is not the most popular of concepts in these enlightened times. Even the writer of the letter to the Hebrews realized that he was courting unpopularity by insisting upon the importance of discipline. He pulls no punches in making his point in his twelfth chapter. The gist of his case is that to be a Christian is to be a son of God, and to be a son is to be under the Father's discipline. Those who are not under the Father's discipline are bastards. But sonship is a relationship into which we have been called by grace. Accordingly, the Father's discipline, though searching, is for our good; it is kindly; the yoke fits snugly;[15] "the Lord disciplines those whom he loves."[16]

Discipline is not only inherent in the status of Christians, however; it is entailed by the work to which they are called. Christians are to be witness-bearers, ambassadors, examples, servants. They must be disciplined for these tasks. They need to be fit. Their bones must be set, their dislocated joints attended to;[17] they are entered for a race which has to be run with perseverance.[18]

More specifically, Christians are under the discipline of the Word of God. This Word, which "cuts more keenly than any two-edged sword,[19] is as searching and challenging when it exhorts to mission as when it spotlights failure. Both those who preach and those who hear are under its discipline. Listen to the seventeenth-century Westminster Larger Catechism on the hearers of the Word:

> It is required of those who hear the Word preached to attend upon it with diligence, preparation, and prayer; examine what they hear by the Scriptures; receive the truth with faith, love, meekness, and readiness of mind, as the Word of God; meditate and speak of it; hide it in their hearts, and bring forth the fruit of it in their lives.[20]

Notice that the Word is to be heard and received by the community. God addresses the corporate priesthood of believers by the Spirit through the Word. If we neglect the communal aspects of Biblical interpretation, in which the checks and balances provided by the insights of all are brought to bear, we shall be in danger of surrendering the Bible to individualists whether of the right or of the left.[21]

Over and above the general discipline under which Christians stand, most branches of the Church have traditionally seen the need for specific disciplining action to be taken from time to time. In this sense the objective has been the building up of the body of Christ by the restoration (ideally), or (sadly) by the withdrawal from, or excommunication of, the erring member or members. There has been concern that weaker brothers and sisters will not be harmed, and that deterrence will do its work.[22] John Knox penned what has become a classic statement on the matter: "as it would be a work both uncharitable and cruel to join together in one bed persons infected with pestilent and other contagious and infected sores, with tender children or such as were sound, so it is no less cruelty to suffer among the flock of Christ such obstinate rebels...for a little leaven corrupteth the whole mass."[23] As to erring members,[24] John Owen made it clear that this meant "the *end* of [discipline] with respect to the *church*, its purging and vindication — with respect unto the person *excommunicated*, his repentance, reformation and salvation..."[25] A further motivation of Church disciplinary activity was that Christ, the holy head of the Church, should not be dishonoured.[26] This was often thought to entail the Christian's not being conformed to the world.[27] Thus, Clement of Alexandria gave pastoral advice to all kinds of people, not excluding the "model maiden" who, he said, will forgo "the wearisome trouble that comes from the shops of perfumers, and goldsmiths, and dealers in wool, and that which comes from the other shops where women, meretriciously dressed, pass whole days as if sitting in the stews."[28] The second generation of Quakers were also keen on this variety of discipline, as when Joseph Pike dispensed with his "fine veneered and garnished cases of drawers,tables, stands, cabinets, escritoires, etc."[29] One hundred years on, the Bible Christian Conference, having noted that the dress of its women preachers was not as plain as hitherto, ruled, "Let them be admonished, and if they will not reform, let them travel no longer."[30] In the wake of the Evangelical Revival some came to feel that God could hardly be expected to revive a undisciplined church: "*The toleration of gross offenses in the Church*, is...[a] serious hindrance to a revival of religion," declared William Sprague.[31]

No doubt there was plenty of room for false legalism, pettiness and downright spite in church disciplinary activity; but at their best the Christians of old knew that the Gospel imposed a discipline on them, that they were to be the Lord's army equipped for battle. Moreover, when they remembered themselves, they knew that they were not the judges. As Robert Browne had said, "by his discipline...he is our king."[32]

In a more general sense, to be committed to any fellowship is to accept the discipline of fellowship. There is certainly pain, frustration and irritation, as well as joy, in the fellowship of the Church. There must be few Christians who have not at some time felt that the Christian pilgrimage would be easier were it not for other Christians. But hear Bernard Manning on this:

> You say you love Christ's Church. Well, here it is: Tom, Dick, Harry, and
> the rest; a funny lot of lame ducks...They are not very good. But they have,

in their own odd ways, heard Christ's call. They have trusted in Christ on His Cross...It is little use your feeling mystical sympathy with St. Francis who is dead, with St. Somebody Else who never existed, with men of good will all over the world whom you are quite safe from meeting. If you do not love your brothers whom you have seen...you cannot, in fact, love those brothers...whom you have not seen.[33]

All of which, as Manning acknowledged, was simply an updating of the seventeenth-century John Owen, who cautioned, "Let none...pretend that they love the brethren in general, and love the people of God, and love the saints, while their love is not fervently exercised towards those who are in the same church society with them. Christ...will try your love at the last day by your deportment in that church wherein you are."[34] This is realistic ecclesiology.

But if, as I said, there are perils to disciplined fellowship from individualism, there are also, in these days, pitfalls in the wrong kind of corporate zeal. There is an important difference between a fellowship of Christians gathered under the gospel, and a corporation run on lines sanctified by the Harvard Business School, and according to which ministers are not so much called as hired and fired; budget and membership growth targets take precedence over praise and prayer; people come to be regarded as so much pew fodder; and ministers are made to compete against colleagues in order not so much to fulfil a vocation as to become the president of a going concern. I once remarked to an American minister that if ever I were visited at my sick bed by a "Senior Executive Pastor" — a title I have seen affixed to doors in some "church plant" — I should jump out of my skin. "Don't worry," replied my friend, "it could not happen: Senior Executive Pastors are only to be found at board meetings and on golf courses." A touch of cynicism, perhaps? Let it be clear that I long for the growth in depth and extent of Christ's Church; administrative efficiency ought to be part of our Christian stewardship. But the model of organizational slickness, of the corporate concern for status (measured by the thickness of the pile on the office carpet), of the *quasi*-commercial concern for better returns this week than we had in the same week last year — this model should at least be questioned by those who see through the tinsel, who know that they are servants, and who recall that, after all, if there is any increase, it is given by God.

 III

From a church whose members are a true fellowship disciplined under the Gospel there will arise heartfelt worship. A whole church — a church of integrity — is a church united in praise. Though quaint to our ears, the Puritan Thomas Watson is very much to the point: "Praise is the quit-rent we pay to God: while God renews our lease, we must renew our rent."[35] The word "worship" means showing what God is worth to us. This presupposes the remembrance of, and gratitude for, his goodness in providence and his grace in redemption. For, as another Puritan, John Flavel, noted "God cannot be glorified for the mercies we never noted."[36]

Time would fail to list all the exhortations to worship which are to be found in the Bible; but they can all be summed up in the resounding affirmation of the Westminster Shorter Catechism: "Man's chief end is to glorify God, and to enjoy him for ever."[37]

But, once again, individualism strikes! Anyone who has braved the rigours of door-to-door evangelism will know that before you have called at six houses you will have met at least one individualistic mystic. These people have no need of fellowship, no need of corporate worship — the presence of others would only disturb their meditation. "I can worship God just as well on a mountain top as I can in church," they say; and their tone of voice often invites the inference that they can worship better on mountain tops than in church, because there are fewer hypocrites on mountain tops. They sometimes proceed to indicate that they have nothing against the teachings of Jesus, but they have no time for the institutional church. Their parting shot may well be, "After all, religion is a personal matter, isn't it?"

Now let us be realistic. In the course of my work I have had the privilege of flying over numerous mountains ranges on clear days. If all the people who say that they can worship there are actually doing it, those places would be more densely populated that they are. No one denies that it is possible to worship God anywhere, but it is also possible to make excuses for worshipping him nowhere. Again, how can people profess to be so enamoured of the teaching of Jesus and then neglect to participate in the very fellowship which he founded, and to which much of his instruction was directed? Certainly religion is a personal matter, but the whole Bible witnesses against the view that it is private. The covenant people, the vine and the branches, the corporate priesthood, the body of Christ — all of these are, as we have seen, social images. God calls out a *people* for his praise and service. Furthermore, he sends them upon a missionary task of such magnitude that it would be the height of arrogance for any individual to suppose that he or she could accomplish it unaided.

But we do not need to go on door-to-door visitations in order to find the individualistic attitude towards worship. We can find it within the church itself. The attitude of consumerism comes into play at this point. The churches are marketing a product, so we think, and we are the consumers. If we seek good music, we go here; if we need a preacher who will keep telling us that we are miserable sinners we go there; if we would be ashamed to use their gymnasium on Wednesdays if we did not put in an appearance on Sundays, we go there. And even if we have a settled Church experience we may be inclined to stay away from worship if the regular preacher is away — or if he is not; or if we know that the organ is under repair and we should have to tolerate the honky-tonk piano from the children's room. We are the customers, and we take it or leave it. How does any of this square with the idea from which I began: that we are to praise God in the company of his people; to *offer*, in the first place, not to take? How shall our churches become centres of pastoral integrity — whole, united fellowships disciplined under the Gospel and ministering to the world around — so long as consumerism prevails in our chief duty which is the praise of God? As P.T. Forsyth wrote, "The greatest product of the Church is not brotherly love but divine worship. And we shall never worship right nor serve right till we are more engrossed with our God than even with our worship, with His reality than our piety, with His Cross than our service."[38]

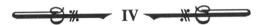

IV

It must by now have struck you that here I am, addressing the question of pastoral integrity, and so far I have said little or nothing about the pastors, the ministers. Instead, I have been speaking about the whole people of God as a serving, caring, disciplined and worshipping community. There are good theological reasons for this. Although in every generation some have been called to the order of ministry, it is not they who create and control the Church. The Church is God's creation, his calling and, in turn, God calls and the Church acknowledges, those who shall be set aside for the order of ministry. This is not the place to discuss in detail the various theories of ordination which have been proposed over the centuries. It is only necessary to underline the fact that in the deepest sense there is only one "essential" ministry in the Church, the perpetual ministry of the Risen and Ever-Present Lord Himself.[39] By the grace of God *all* Christians are caught up in that ministry. There is thus something misleading about the familiar clergy/laity distinction. No doubt in some contexts the distinction is convenient, and I am certainly not saying that God's call to the ordered ministry of Word and Sacraments is unimportant. But, on the one hand, we must not so elevate ministers, or abstract them, that they no longer belong to the people. On the other hand, we must not so exalt the ordained ministers, or professionalize them, as to downplay the ministry of everybody else. If you do not care for the theology, consider the history.

It is not without significance, and it is humbling to the ordained, that some of the most important advances of the Church have occurred without them. In the early days of the Church there were such appointed evangelists as Philip, who went out on deliberate missions. We are told that Philip went around proclaiming the Messiah; and the Greek word used for his proclaiming means heralding. There was something official about it. But in the previous verse in Acts 8, we read of persecuted Christians, who were driven from their homes following the stoning of Stephen. They, we learn, "went through the country preaching the Word" and the word used for their preaching means "gossiping." In their unofficial capacity they gossiped the Gospel — and with considerable success: "a great many became believers, and turned to the Lord."[40] Moreover, these gossipers of the Gospel did more than anyone else to spread the Word in the early centuries. As T.W. Manson explained, "The great preachers came after Constantine the Great; and before that Christianity had already done its work and made its way right through the Empire from end to end. When we try to picture how it was done we seem to see domestic servants teaching Christ in and through their domestic service, workers doing it through their work, small shopkeepers through their trade, and so on, rather than eloquent propagandists swaying mass meetings of interested inquirers."[41]

But, it might be said, those were early days, and once things became settled with regular orders of ministry, there was a change. No doubt there have been Roman priests and Protestant "princes of the pulpit" who have, to their shame, tried to make ministry their exclusive preserve, but every so often circumstances have given the people back their opportunity. Consider just one example: during the English Civil War of the seventeenth century Walter Cradock of Llanvaches, and other ministers, had to flee from South Wales to the relative security of London. In a sermon published in 1648 he said,

> I have observed, and seen, in the Mountains of Wales [that] the Gospel is run over the Mountaines between Brecknockshire and Monmouthshire, as the fire in the thatch; and who should doe this? They have no ministers: but some of the wisest say, there are about eight hundred godly people, and they goe from one to another. They have no ministers, it is true; if they had, they would honour them and blesse God for them: and shall we raile at such, and say they are Tubpreachers, and they were never at the University? Let us fall downe, and honour God;...They were filled with good newes, and they tell it to others.[42]

To repeat: I mention all of this not in order to disparage the ordered ministry. There is a proper place for leadership in the Church, provided it be modelled after the style of the Lord of the Church, who took a towel and washed his disciples' feet.[43] I do, however, believe that Daniel Jenkins is on good biblical and theological ground when he writes, "The primary human reality in the Church is not the ministry but the...common life of the people of God...if the apostles were meant to represent Israel, all who belong to Israel share in their succession."[44]

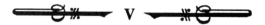

V

So much by way of preamble to my next main point: if our objective, under God, is churches which are whole centres of pastoral love and care, we shall be greatly helped if our ministers are whole people fulfilling a whole ministry.

Whole ministers are confident, though not arrogant, in their calling. They are sustained by those who have called them; they are nourished by their devotional life. I could extend this description, but I need not. Rather, I wish to comment upon those ministers who are not whole. We hear much at the present time concerning what is called ministerial burn out. This is an increasingly widespread condition, it knows no denominational boundaries, and it is serious. It is serious for the burnt-out minister; it is serious for the whole Church.

No doubt a certain nervous tension accompanies any creative activity. Actors and musicians experience it, and so do teachers and ministers. But it is one thing to experience that heightening of tension which gears one up for the task in hand; it is quite another to be paralyzed by anxiety.

Again, it is right that ministers and others should feel *distress* at some things. To be "hail-fellow-well-met" and bouncing with *bonhomie* in all conceivable situations can be downright cruelty to others. Some situations are desperately sad. George Herbert knew this well, and in his advice to country parsons he said that the country parson "meets continually with two most sad spectacles, Sin, and Misery; God dishonoured every day, and man afflicted."[45] But if there is a proper distress, there is also an unhealthy stress which saps vitality, evaporates joy and disturbs peace. Why does it arise? In some cases the causes seem to contextual. It has been observed that ministers pioneering in new areas are especially at risk. According to a recent article, "On top of the burdens any cleric carries, a minister in a new church faces the demoralizing prospect of preaching temporarily in a school cafeteria, rounding up new members, riding shotgun over construction crews, organizing neophyte church workers into committees and referring squabbles that inevitably arise."[46] But there are many more widespread and more subtle causes too, and from these I selected two for mention.

I think it may truthfully be said that in some parts of the West a crisis of confidence in ministry as such developed during the 1960s and 1970s. If I may put the matter briefly and bluntly: there was, among other factors, a good deal of less-than-bolstering theology — *Honest to God*, the death of God — and some ministers wondered what they could now preach about with confidence. If they thought they knew what needed to said, then educational theorists came along and tried to gag them as far as children were concerned. By an abuse of Piaget, many came to feel that until a child was "ready," or had the appropriate "concept" it was damaging to mention certain things — like God, for example. Perhaps I caricature a little, but I did hear some very odd theorizing in those days! With shaky theology and inhibiting educational theory, it is not surprising that some ministers thought that there must be *something* they could usefully do, so many took themselves off into social work, or found specialist positions in church structures which would insulate them to some extent from some of the problems. Many ministers felt that they had to be seen to be busy all over the place, and some still feel this way. A correspondent in a church magazine of July 1988 summed up matters nicely. The minister, he wrote, "does too many things, and so does them badly. He feels guilty when he spends time in his study and may well become a stranger to it. This also makes him...a stranger to the presence of God...The result of this is increasing stress, increasing manse marital break-up, and an increasing number of young ministers leaving their vocation while in their first charges."[47]

The crisis in confidence in ministry is often accompanied by increased concern for ministerial status. Ministers feel they must count for something. Sometimes ministers and churches aid and abet one another in this matter. The church members say, "The neighbouring church has a minister with a doctorate — we must see that our minister secures a D.Min." Or the minister will think, "If I obtain a Doctorate in Ministry, I shall be well placed for my next career [note the word] move: I may even land a 'tall steeple church.' " I assure you that I am not simply fantasizing — and I do not wish to be misunderstood. I am entirely in favour of schemes which ensure that ministers open books and reflect theologically and in depth upon their work. I am simply calling into question some ways of thinking about the ordered ministry which owe more to the world's notions of success than to the Bible's concept of vocation, and which have the capacity to undermine the true relation of pastor and people and so to militate against ecclesial integrity.

Let me offer one illustration. A minister said to me in all seriousness, "If my wife and I did not both drive the largest limousines, my elders would not respect us at all — they would think we were the caretakers." Now the God of the elders, as we know, is no respecter of persons; but it would seem that those elders think in terms of a clear pecking order, expect their minister to conform to it, and judge him accordingly. How far these status notions seem from the idea of the pastor-people relationship as being forged by Christ and analogous to marriage. As Robert Paul wrote, " In various ways the Minister proclaims the love of God in Christ, but in the deepest sense the relationship of a Minister to the congregation he serves, and of the people's relationship to him, must exemplify the love which they proclaim."[48] And that love is self-effacing, non-status-seeking, serving love.

Please do not think that I am acquiescing in the *ill*-treatment of ministers. There is a hoary English tale concerning an eighteenth-century fund which was established to benefit "poor and godly" ministers. One day a group of elders was considering applying to the fund in order to augment their minister's stipend. The possibility was scotched when one prominent elder declared, "We can trust the Lord to make him godly, and we'll keep him poor." The tales of some of the ministers of those days pacing their studies while thinking out their sermons, because they could not afford to heat their manses, make harrowing reading.

But if faulty less-than fully-*vocational* goals can lead to stress and burnout, so can faulty expectations. If both minister and people — or either party — think that it is the minister's task to build up the church unaided; and if building up the church is taken to mean such quantitative matters as increasing the income and the membership; then, if these signs of "success" are not forthcoming, trouble looms ahead. What is required is a serious questioning of the concept of success. Pastor and people are not called to be successful in those quasi-commercial terms, but to be obedient. We have no obligation to devise bigger and better stunts, or to stage-manage ever greater spiritual thrills in order to meet goals of that kind — still less in order to outdo our ecclesiastical competitors. "What we must deliver ourselves from," writes Daniel Jenkins, "is the notion expressed by many enthusiastic spirits in these days, that the Gospel is not triumphantly spread abroad simply because we fail to 'sell' it effectively enough and that all we need to be is more energetic, dynamic, up to date and super-efficient."[49] As P.T. Forsyth declared, "Our first business is neither to gather men nor to move them, but to preach...the universal and moving Gospel. Let *it* gather them, and let *it* stir them."[50] And the Baptist preacher C.H. Spurgeon reminded his students that "The minister, whose whole year's work ended with one convert, and that one was Robert Moffat [the celebrated missionary to Africa], did not reap a scanty harvest."[51]

What is further required is that we recall our theology. God is sovereign in salvation; he, not we ourselves, is Lord of the harvest. It is ours to proclaim, it is his to save. As that wise Puritan Thomas Watson pointed out, "The ministers of God are only the pipes and organs; it is the Spirit blowing in them, that effectually changes the heart."[52] Neither churches nor ministers should forget that. The strains of amnesia can be colossal. If ministers or churches or both really think that the minister alone carries the responsibility where church growth is concerned, it is not surprising that burnout sometimes ensues. The ministry of proclamation and pastoral care is the task of pastor and people together, but God gives any increase. I will say no more on this, except to ask you to hear, as a cautionary tale, this extract from the diary of Jean Frederic Oberlin who, during the eighteenth century, ministered for fifty years in Waldbach, Alsace:

> The pastor of Waldbach, if he tries to be what he ought to be in this vast parish — is a poor dog, a beast of burden, a cart-horse. He must do everything... Everything sits upon the pastor who meets everywhere nothing but hindrance, obstacles, delays, and red-tape; and not being able to please everybody must fight constantly with malevolence.[53]

It is comforting to ministers to recall with James Denney that "there were people with whom even Paul...could not prevail. There were people who hardened their hearts against Christ; and let the preacher be ever so unworthy of the gospel, the virtue is in it, and not in him."[54]

In the last resort the only way a minister will retain integrity — that is, be a whole person — is as he or she lives in and by the Gospel they are called to proclaim. Spurgeon was his usual blunt self: "We may not be butchers at the block chopping off for hungry ones the meat of which we do not partake."[55] Two centuries earlier Richard Baxter warned pastors to "take heed to yourselves lest you perish while you call on others to take heed of perishing."[56] George Herbert said that the faithful pastor "sucks and lives" in the Bible;[57] and did not Martin Luther somewhere say, "I have so many things to do today that I must spend several hours in prayer?"

One day a young minister, recently arrived in the parish, went to visit the most eminent parishioner, Thomas Carlyle. After some general conversation the minister asked, "What do you think this parish most needs in its minister?" Carlyle's reply was quick: "What this parish needs is a man who knows God otherwise than by hearsay."[58] Such a minister is a minister of integrity — wholeness. So to my last point.

 VI

Whole ministers will be able to perform a whole ministry. They will see the connection between the preaching office and the pastoral office. For how can you regularly preach to the needs of people if you do not know them? What are you doing in pastoral visits if you never communicate the gospel? I know very well that in these days some ministers are called to special tasks; they become specialists in Christian education, or church administration, and their opportunities of performing a regular preaching and pastoral ministry are gone. By all means let ministers use their gifts as they feel led and as the Church authorizes them. But let them never despise the pastoral ministry (as some are inclined to do); for that ministry is still at the front line of Christian witness and service. If specialist ministers feel that they are at a frontier (and they may well be), let them not forget that the local pastor can, under God, inspire and equip as many frontiersmen and women as the Church he or she serves has members. The words of my teacher Gordon Rupp are worthy of recall at this point:

> I have stuck my own neck out as far as the next man's to get young men set aside for experimental and new ministries, as an urgent priority of the Churches' mission. But I sometimes wonder whether some of them are not anxious to be involved in everything except chores, like learning N.T. Greek, or visiting the flock in hospital, or sweating away at sermons...there is in the end no substitution for this one essential ministry of the Church, the shepherding of souls, in the time of their wealth and of their tribulation, at the moments of birth and marriage and in the article of death.[59]

This is not the place to treat the nature and scope of the preaching and pastoral ministry in depth: that is a huge project. I wish only to make one thing clear: the minister of integrity will ground all of his or her work in a deeply-held theological perspective. The work as a whole will be informed by a theological vision, which is to say, by the vision of God. Without this deep root the ministry will flounder — however superficially successful it may appear. I once asked the minister of a very large church — a church with a large supporting staff, with more than one choir, with numerous organizations and a huge set of premises, what was the thing which held his ministry together. I wondered if there might be some theological thread to it all. By way of reply he took me into his computer room and dazzled me with technology.

What might be among the ingredients of a theologically-grounded vision? Some of the basic Christian doctrines will suggest clues to an answer. Think, for example, of the transcendence and immanence of God. These themes are epitomized in the vision of Isaiah of Jerusalem,[60] who found that the transcendent, high and holy God, was also uncomfortably close, so that penitence was required. In public worship, do our people feel that they have been in the presence of such a God? Are they even encouraged to think that there is such a God into whose presence they may come? Or do they experience something akin to a happy social hour, or an hour sitting in a freezer? What has been the thrust of the Word proclaimed? Was it more to do with sin and misery than with grace? Was Christ proclaimed at all — and if so, was he proclaimed as Master, Teacher, or Saviour? Did the preacher glory in the Cross, or revel in his dialectical skills and oratorical devices? Was there both a proclamation of good news and a challenge to amendment of life? Certainly, the Gospel is not a new legalism: it is about freedom from bondage; but those thus freed should love the law of the Lord. The themes of both grace and law need to be within the preacher's purview. No on knew better than Thomas Watson how difficult it was to strike all the right balances. He confessed, "There are two things, which I have always looked upon as difficult. The one is, to make the wicked sad; the other is, to make the godly joyful."[61] Only on the basis of an integrated theological perspective can the task even begin.

Again, is the life of the local church guided by a vision of its missionary task, or is the church seen as a collection of miscellaneous and sometimes competing organizations? Yet again, what of the specific pastoral work of the church? What will ministers say at a member's death bed? If they have any sense they will not begin with "Now let us consider the following three theories of immortality..." But they will have so reflected upon the issues of life and death, and upon the victory of Christ, that they will be able to speak words of comfort and hope which will, by the Holy Spirit, become more than hollow platitudes.

Pastoral guidance is a complex matter. Here too firm rootage in a theological foundation is necessary. We must not let humanist psychotherapists have it all their own way. Some of them tell us that the only proper counselling is non-directive counselling: we must not appear to be advising, still less judging. Now certainly, a person needs to come to his or her own decisions in his or her own time and way; and we are not the judges of others. But when non-directive becomes non-responsive we are behaving in a less-than-human manner; and as for judgment, we cannot obliterate the concept from Christian thought even though we are not sitting in judgment on our fellows. For Christians, judgment is a concept with a constellation of concepts of which the first and last are grace and mercy.

Finally, how can anyone offer pastoral care except in the light of a doctrine of humanity, which may not always be articulated, but is always presupposed in any pastoral activity? Every counselling theory presupposes a doctrine of humanity. I was pleased to find that the psychologist, J.A.C. Brown, confirms my view: "Although all schools of psychology dealing with the total personality claim to be wholly scientific and to have based their theories solely upon hard facts and the results of experiments or dispassionate observations, this is not in fact true, since they inevitably begin with a belief about man's essential nature which forms the implicit frame of reference into which their faith and the results of their observations are fitted rather than the reverse, as they would have us believe."[62]

Accordingly, if you view your counselling in a theological perspective you will understand that the troubled person is created in God's image; that is, he or she has an inherent worth, and is capable of fellowship with God; you will know that there is the possibility of redemption, and that there are resources of hope, joy and peace in the Gospel, and the prospect of loving fellowship in the church. In a nutshell, in Christ there is integrity, wholeness, to be found. Our conviction on this point cannot but influence the way in which we view others, and the steps we take to minister to them.

 VII

When you have churches which are true fellowships, disciplined for mission and united in worship; when such churches are ministered to by whole ministers performing a whole ministry anchored in the Gospel of the grace of God, then you have pastoral centres of health and healing, of honesty and wholeness, of integrity. Since the churches are composed of the likes of us, they will never be more than earthen vessels. But we can have clarity as to our objectives and understanding of the steps necessary to the, at least partial, attainment of those objectives. Moreover, we have One beside us as we go, who picks us up when we stumble, and who calls us back when we stray. This is enough. We may leave the final issue where it belongs — with God.

NOTES

1. *The Journal of George Fox*, ed. John L. Nickalls (London: Religious Society of Friends, 1975), 5–6.

2. Tertullian, *Apologeticus*, XXXIX.

3. See John 15:5.

4. See I Corinthians 12.

5. See I Peter 2: 9.

6. Exodus 19:6.

7. Amos 3: 2.

8. Luke 6: 46.

9. Quoted by Gordon Rupp, *The Righteousness of God* (London: Hodder & Stoughton, 1953), 316.

10. *The School of Faith. The Catechisms of the Reformed Church*, ed. T.F. Torrance (London: James Clarke, 1959), 11. On the general question of the priesthood of all believers see G.D. Henderson, "Priesthood of Believers," *Scottish Journal of Theology* VII (1954): 1–15; John R. Crawford, "Calvin and the Priesthood of all Believers," ibid., XXI (1968): 145–156.

11. Thomas M. Lindsay, *A History of the Reformation*, 2nd ed. (Edinburgh: T. & T. Clark, 1907), I: 444.

12. Peter J. Drilling, "Common and Ministerial Priesthood: *Lumen Gentium*, Article Ten," *The Irish Theological Quarterly* LIII (1987): 95.

13. T.W. Manson, *Ministry and Priesthood: Christ's and Ours* (London: Epworth Press, 1958), 85.

14. P.J. Drilling, op.cit., 85.

15. See Matthew 11: 30.

16. Hebrews 12: 6; cf. Proverbs 3:12.

17. See Hebrews 12: 12, 13.

18. Ibid., 12: 1.

19. Ibid., 4: 12.

20. *Westminster Larger Catechism*, Q & A 160.

21. See Gabriel Fackre, *The Christian Story. A Pastoral Systematics* (Grand Rapids: Eerdmans, 1987), II, 222–26, for the place of the ecclesial community in biblical interpretation.

22. I Corinthians 8: 9; I Timothy v: 20.

23. John Knox, *Order of Excommunication*, Ch. 3.

24. II Thessalonians 3: 14; I Corinthians 5: 2; Matthew 18: 15; II Corinthians 2: 6–8; Galatians 6: 1.

25. J. Owen, *The True Nature of a Gospel Church*, *Works*, ed. William H. Goold, (1850–3; reprint, London: The Banner of Truth Trust, 1968), XVI: 161.

26. Romans 2: 23.

27. Romans 12: 2.

28. Clement of Alexandria, *Paedagogus*, III, xi.

29. See his *Life*, 1837; and on the entire subject, William C. Braithwaite, *The Second Period of Quakerism*, 2nd ed. (Cambridge: Cambridge University Press, 1961), Ch. XVIII.

30. *Minutes* of the Bible Christian Conference, 1824.

31. William Sprague, *Lectures on Revivals*, (1832; reprint, Edinburgh: The Banner of Truth Trust, 1959), 73.

32. R. Browne, *An Answer to Master Cartwright His Letter* (1858?) in *The Writings of Robert Harrison and Robert Browne*, ed. A. Peel and Leland H. Carlson (London: Allen & Unwin, 1953), 461.

33. B.L. Manning, *Why Not Abandon the Church?* (1939; reprint, London: Independent Press, 1958), 37–8.

34. J. Owen, Sermon XXI, "Gospel Charity," *Works*, IX: 262.

35. Thomas Watson, *A Body of Divinity*, (1692: reprint, London: The Banner of Truth Trust, 1965), 15.

36. John Flavel, *Works*, (1820: reprint, London: The Banner of Truth Trust, 1968), IV: 448.

37. *Westminster Shorter Catechism*, A. I.

38. P.T. Forsyth, *The Church and the Sacraments*, (1917; reprint, London: Independent press, 1947), 25. For Canadian religious consumerism see Reginald W. Bibby, *Fragmented Gods* (Toronto: Irwin, 1987), Chs. IV, VI.

39. T.W. Manson, *The Church's Ministry* (London: Hodder & Stoughton, 1948), 100; cf. 21.

40. Acts 11: 21.

41. T.W. Manson, *Ministry and Priesthood*, 21. He adds, "It is still true that the best propaganda for genuine Christianity is genuine Christians."

42. Walter Cradock, *Glad Tidings from Heaven to the Worst Sinners on Earth, 1648*, quoted by H. Elvet Lewis, *Nonconformity in Wales* (London: National Council of Evengelical Free Churches, [1904]), 21.

43. John 13: 3–17.

44. Daniel Jenkins, *The Protesant Ministry* (London: Faber, 1958), 34.

45. George Herbert, *The Country Parson and Selected Poems* (London: SCM Press, 1956), 70.

46. Stephen Nicholls, "Churches Struggle with Clergy Burnout," *Calgary Herald*, 16 April 1988.

47. Gilbert L. Thompson, *Life and Work* [Church of Scotland], July 1988, 34.

48. Robert S. Paul, *Ministry* (Grand Rapids: Eerdmans, 1965), 120.

49. Daniel Jenkins, *The Gift of Ministry* (London: Faber, 1957), 135.

50. P.T. Forsyth, *The Church, The Gospel and Society* (London: Independent Press, 1962), 115.

51. C.H. Spurgeon, *An All-Round Ministry* (1900; reprint, London: The Banner of Truth Trust, 1960), 77.

52. Thomas Watson, *A Divine Cordial* (1663; reprint, Grand Rapids: Sovereign Grace, 1971), 78.

53. Quoted by Robert G. Dickson, "Ministering to the Minister: Formulating a Programme," *Reformed Review* XXXI (2, Winter 1978): 88.

54. James Denney, *The Epistles to the Thessalonians* (London: Hodder & Stoughton, 1897), 49.

55. C.H. Spurgeon, op.cit., 66.

56. R. Baxter, *The Reformed Pastor* (1656; reprint, London: SCM Press, 1956), 28.

57. G. Herbert, *The Country Parson*, 16.

58. Quoted by Alan Flavell, "The place of the Evangelical in the Church of Today," *The Monthly Record of the Free Church of Scotland*, January 1969, 14.

59. Gordon Rupp, *The Old Reformation and the New* (London: Epworth, 1967), 55.

60. Isaiah 6.

61. Thomas Watson, *A Divine Cordial*, preface.

62. J.A.C. Brown, *Freud and the Post-Freudians* (Harmondsworth: Pelican, 1965), 15.

INDEX

INDEX OF PERSONS

INDEX OF SUBJECTS